The Complete
SLOW COOKER
Collection

50 Effortless Recipes for Heartwarming
Home-Cooked Meals Across the Globe

James Stott

Copyright © James Stott 2024

All rights reserved. No part of this publication may be reproduced, distributed, or transmitted in any form or by any means, including photocopying, recording, or other electronic or mechanical methods, without the prior written permission of the publisher, except in the case of brief quotations embodied in critical reviews and certain other noncommercial uses permitted by copyright law.

> We really hope that you enjoy this culinary adventure and would ask that if you are enjoying the recipes here that you consider placing a review or star rating on Amazon using the link or QR code below. Your review really helps others to find this book and it would be really appreciated.

INTRODUCTION

Welcome to "The Complete Slow Cooker Collection," your definitive guide to mastering the art of slow-cooked, savory meals that warm the heart and comfort the soul. Within these pages lies a curated selection of 50 recipes that showcase the magic of the slow cooker, offering you a passport to explore a world of rich flavors and tender textures with minimal effort.

This book is a celebration of the slow cooker's ability to transform everyday ingredients into extraordinary meals. Whether you're a novice in the kitchen seeking to expand your culinary skills or a seasoned cook looking for new inspirations, this collection is designed to suit all tastes and lifestyles. From the robust, hearty stews that have long been slow cooker staples to innovative dishes that bring global cuisines right to your table, every recipe is an adventure waiting to be savored.

"The Complete Slow Cooker Collection" emphasizes the diversity and versatility of slow cooking. Here, you'll find everything from the tender pull-apart textures of Crockpot Beef Chili to the subtly spiced and aromatic Slow Cooker Vegetable Curry. Each recipe has been chosen for its simplicity, flavor, and the joy it brings to those who share in the meal.

Beyond just recipes, this book is a guide to embracing the convenience and depth of flavor that slow cooking offers. It's about coming home to a perfectly cooked meal, about spending less time in the kitchen while still enjoying delicious, home-cooked dinners every night. With tips on how to get the most out of your slow cooker, variations to tailor dishes to your taste, and insights into the ingredients that make each recipe special, you're equipped to make every meal a success.

Join us on a culinary journey that promises to enrich your meal times with ease and flavor. Let "The Complete Slow Cooker Collection" transform the way you cook, bringing you closer to the world of comforting, homemade meals that await with the simple turn of your slow cooker's knob. Welcome to your new favorite way to dine at home. Let's begin this delicious adventure together.

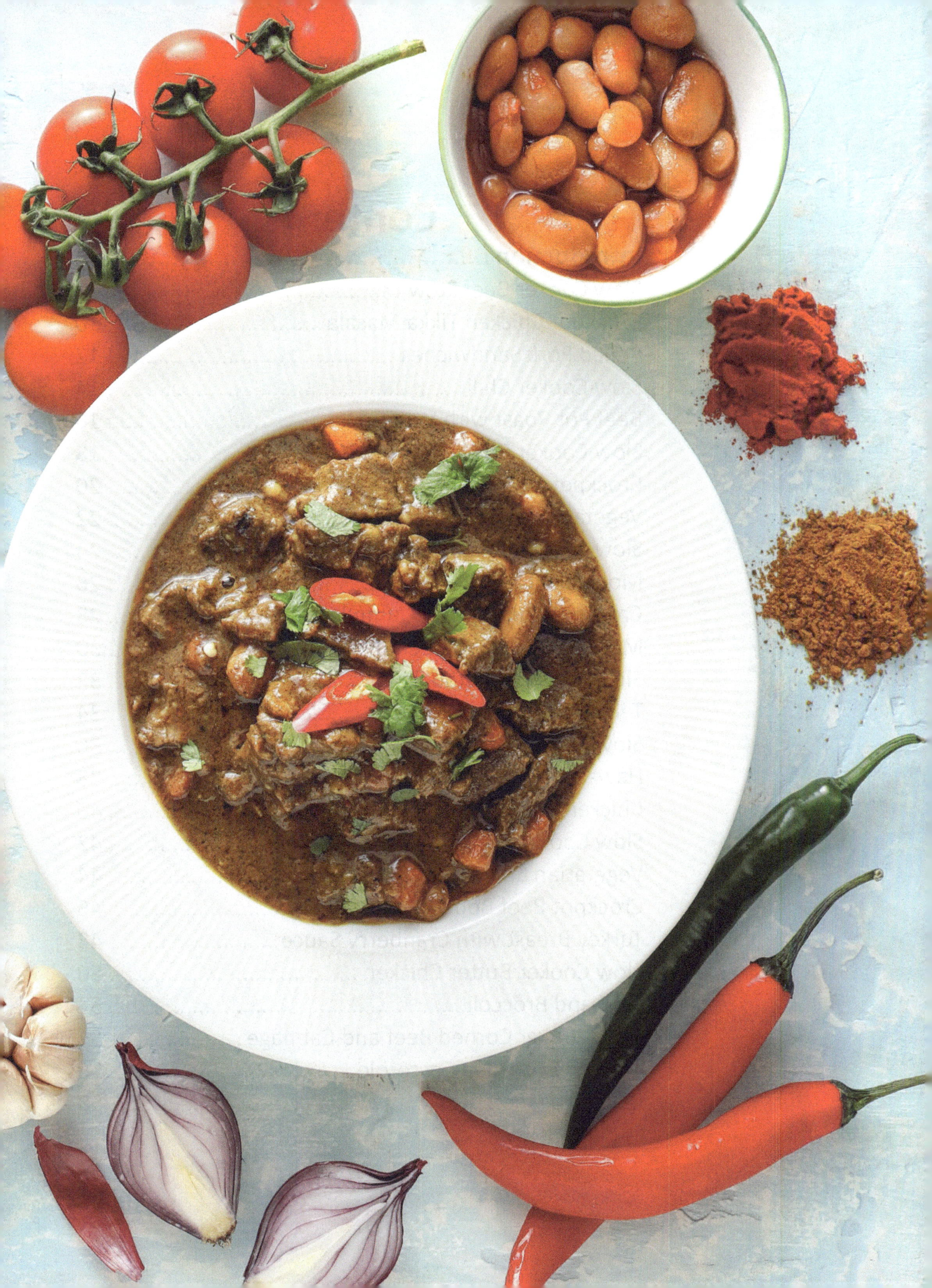

Contents

Introduction 4
Slow Cooker Beef Stew 8
Crockpot Chicken Tikka Masala 10
Pulled Pork Sandwiches 12
Slow Cooker Chili 14
Beef Pot Roast with Vegetables 16
Slow Cooker Chicken Fajitas 18
Crockpot BBQ Ribs 20
Vegetable Soup 22
Slow Cooker Spaghetti Bolognese 24
Moroccan Lamb Tagine 26
Crockpot Chicken and Dumplings 28
Mexican Shredded Beef for Tacos 30
Slow Cooker Ratatouille 32
Teriyaki Chicken 34
Slow Cooker Lentil Soup 36
Hawaiian Pulled Pork 38
Chicken Cacciatore 40
Slow Cooker Jambalaya 42
Vegetarian Chili 44
Crockpot Beef Bourguignon 46
Turkey Breast with Cranberry Sauce 48
Slow Cooker Butter Chicken 50
Beef and Broccoli 52
Slow Cooker Corned Beef and Cabbage 54
Chicken Enchilada Casserole 56
Beef Stroganoff 58

Slow Cooker Chicken Curry 60
Macaroni and Cheese 62
Slow Cooker Pork Carnitas 64
Sweet and Sour Meatballs 66
Mediterranean Chicken with Olives and Tomatoes 68
Crockpot Beef Stroganoff 70
Slow Cooker Chicken Parmesan 72
Beef and Guinness Stew 74
Slow Cooker Thai Peanut Chicken 76
Vegetarian Sloppy Joes 78
Slow Cooker Chicken Teriyaki 80
Crockpot Chicken Alfredo Pasta 82
Slow Cooker Ratatouille 84
Buffalo Chicken Dip 86
Slow Cooker Chicken and Rice 88
Slow Cooker Vegetarian Lasagna 90
BBQ Pulled Chicken 92
Slow Cooker Beef Tacos 94
Creamy Tortellini Soup 96
Lemon Garlic Chicken 98
Crockpot Lasagna 100
Slow Cooker Chicken Tacos 102
Crockpot Beef Chili 104
Slow Cooker Vegetable Curry 106

Conclusion **108**

SLOW COOKER BEEF STEW

INGREDIENTS

- 2 lb. beef stew meat, cubed
- 1/4 cup all-purpose flour
- 1/2 teaspoon salt
- 1/2 teaspoon ground black pepper
- 2 tablespoons olive oil
- 1 onion, chopped
- 2 cloves garlic, minced
- 2 cups beef broth
- 1 tablespoon tomato paste
- 1 teaspoon Worcestershire sauce
- 1 teaspoon dried thyme
- 2 bay leaves
- 3 carrots, peeled and sliced
- 2 potatoes, peeled and cubed
- 1 cup frozen peas (add in the last hour of cooking)

Prep Time: 20 mins   **Cook Time: 8 hours**   **Serving: 6**

INSTRUCTIONS

1. In a large, deep-bottom bowl, combine the flour, salt, and crushed pepper. Add beef pieces and toss to coat evenly.
2. Heat two tbsp oil in a skillet over medium heat. Add meat pieces in batches, browning on all sides. Transfer the seared meat cubes to the slow cooker.
3. In the same skillet, add the onion and garlic. Sauté until softened, about 2-3 minutes. Transfer to the slow cooker.
4. To the slow cooker, ladle in beef broth, tomato paste, Worcestershire sauce, dried thyme, and bay leaves. Stir to combine.
5. Add carrot slices and potatoes cubeses to the slow cooker. Stir to mix well.
6. Cover and cook on low for 8 hours or high for 4 hours.
7. In the last hour of cooking, add the frozen peas and remove the bay leaves.
8. Serve hot, and enjoy your hearty beef stew.

Nutritional Values (per serving):

Calories: 350, Protein: 35g, Carbohydrate: 24g, Fat: 12g

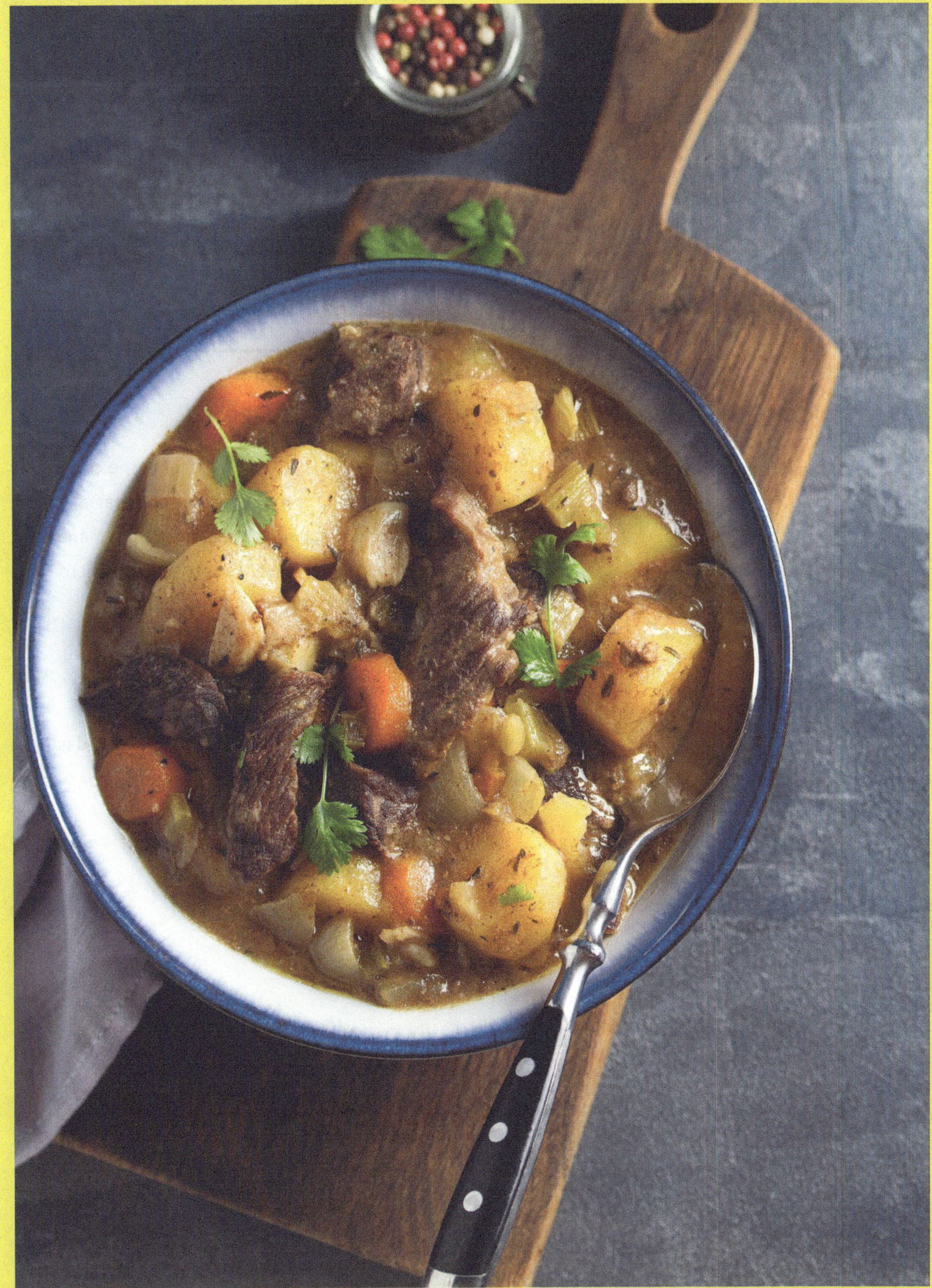

CROCKPOT CHICKEN TIKKA MASALA

Prep Time: 15 mins **Cook Time: 6 hours** **Serving: 6**

INGREDIENTS

- 2 lbs without skin & bone chicken thighs cut into bite-sized pieces
- 1 large onion, finely chopped
- 4 garlic cloves, minced
- 2 tablespoons fresh ginger, grated
- 1 can (14 oz) diced tomatoes
- 1 can (14 oz) coconut milk
- 3 tablespoons tomato paste
- 2 tablespoons garam masala
- 1 teaspoon turmeric
- 1 teaspoon cumin
- 1 teaspoon paprika
- 1/2 teaspoon cayenne pepper (adjust to taste)
- Salt to taste
- 1 cup frozen peas
- Fresh cilantro for garnish
- Cooked rice for serving

INSTRUCTIONS

1. Place the chicken, onion, garlic, and ginger in the crockpot.
2. Mix the diced tomatoes, coconut milk, tomato paste, garam masala, turmeric, cumin, paprika, cayenne pepper, and salt in a bowl. Pour this mixture over the chicken in the crockpot and stir to combine.
3. Cover and cook on low flame/heat for 6 hours.
4. Stir in the frozen peas 30 minutes before the end of cooking time.
5. Serve the Chicken Tikka Masala over cooked rice and garnish with fresh cilantro.

Nutritional Values (per serving):

Calories: 420, Protein: 28g, Carbohydrate: 20g, Fat: 27g

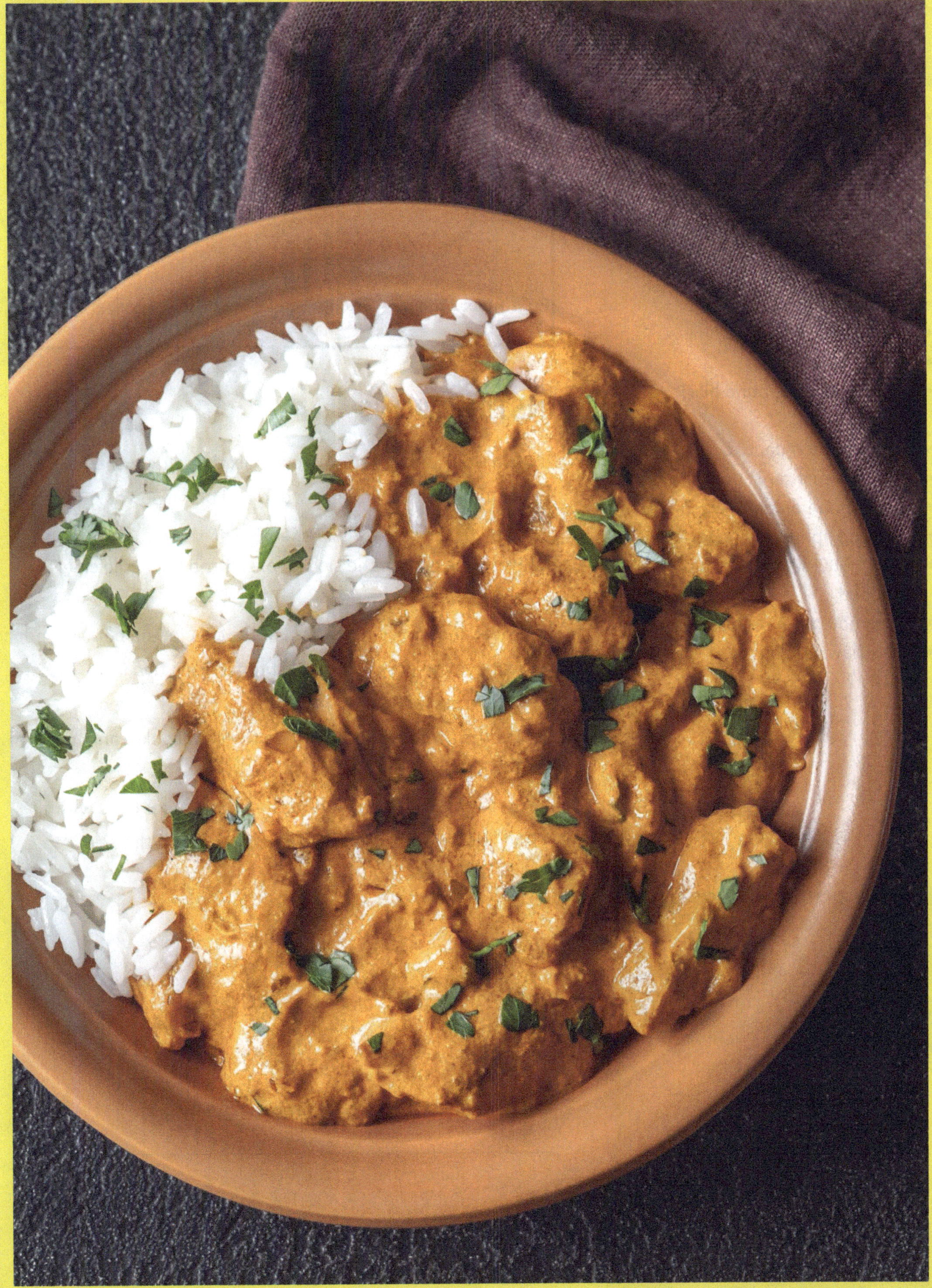

PULLED PORK SANDWICHES

Prep Time: 10 mins **Cook Time:** 8 hours **Serving:** 8

INGREDIENTS

- 4 lbs pork shoulder
- 1 tablespoon salt
- 1 tablespoon ground black pepper
- 1 tablespoon paprika
- 2 teaspoons garlic powder
- 1 teaspoon onion powder
- 1/2 cup apple cider vinegar
- 1 cup BBQ sauce, plus more if needed
- 8 hamburger buns, toasted
- Coleslaw, for serving

INSTRUCTIONS

1. In a small, deep-bottom bowl, mix the salt, crushed pepper, paprika, garlic powder, and onion powder. Rub this seasoning all over the pork shoulder.
2. Place the pork in the slow cooker. Drop the apple cider vinegar around the pork.
3. Cover and cook on low for 8 hours or until the pork is tender.
4. Remove the pork meat and shred it using two forks. Discard any excess fat.
5. Put the shredded pork back to the slow cooker and mix with 1 cup barbecue sauce.
6. Serve the pulled pork on toasted hamburger buns with additional barbecue sauce and coleslaw on the side.

Nutritional Values (per serving):

Calories: 690, Protein: 48g, Carbohydrate: 40g, Fat: 35g

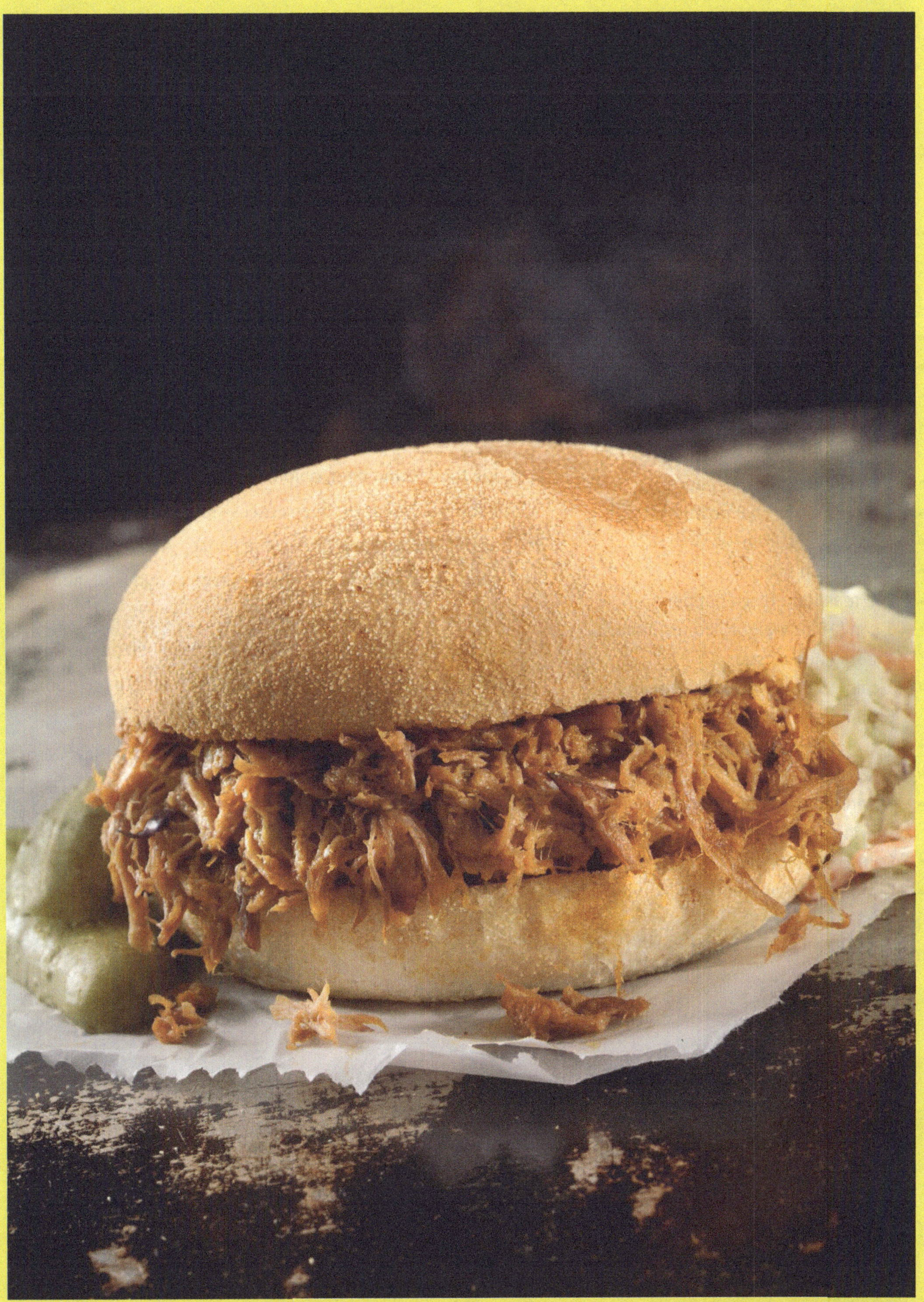

SLOW COOKER CHILI

Prep Time: 20 mins **Cook Time:** 8 hours **Serving:** 8

INGREDIENTS

- 2 lbs ground beef
- 1 onion, chopped
- 2 cloves garlic, minced
- 1 can (28 oz) diced tomatoes, undrained
- 1 can (15 oz) tomato sauce
- 2 tablespoons chili powder
- 1 teaspoon cumin
- 1 teaspoon salt
- 1/2 teaspoon black pepper
- 1 can (15 oz weight) kidney beans, drained and rinsed
- 1 can (15 oz weight) black beans, drained and rinsed
- 1 green bell pepper, chopped
- 1 red bell pepper, chopped
- Shredded cheddar cheese for serving
- Sour cream for serving
- Chopped green onions for serving

INSTRUCTIONS

1. Cook the ground beef, onion, and garlic in a skillet until the meat is browned. Drain any excess fat.
2. Transfer the beef mixture to the cooker. Add diced tomatoes, tomato sauce, chili powder, cumin, salt, and pepper. Stir to combine.
3. Add the kidney beans, black beans, green bell pepper, and red bell pepper to the slow cooker. Stir again to incorporate all the ingredients.
4. Cover and cook on low for 8 hours, allowing the flavors to meld together.
5. Serve it with shredded cheese, sour cream, and chopped green onions.

Nutritional Values (per serving):

Calories: 350, Protein: 26g, Carbohydrate: 24g, Fat: 18g

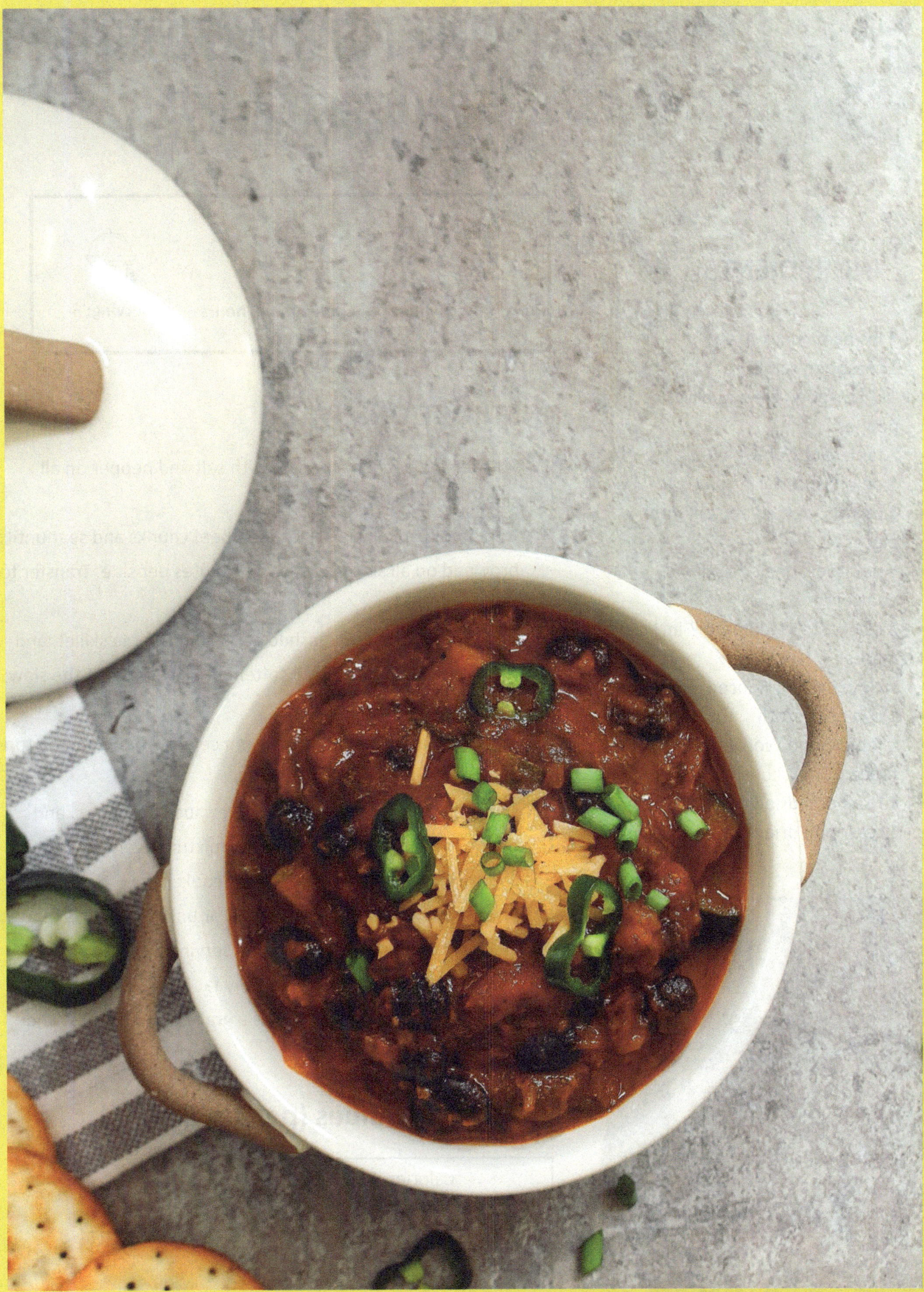

BEEF POT ROAST WITH VEGETABLES

Prep Time: 20 mins   **Cook Time:** 8 hours   **Serving:** 6

INGREDIENTS

- 3 lbs beef chuck roast
- 1 teaspoon salt
- 1/2 teaspoon ground black pepper
- 2 tablespoons olive oil
- 1 onion, sliced
- 4 carrots, peeled and cut into pieces
- 4 potatoes, peeled and quartered
- 2 celery stalks, cut into 2-inch pieces
- 3 cloves garlic, minced
- 1 cup beef broth
- 1 tablespoon Worcestershire sauce
- 1 teaspoon dried rosemary
- 1 teaspoon dried thyme

INSTRUCTIONS

1. Powder the beef chuck roast with salt and pepper on all sides.
2. Heat two tbsp oil in a skillet. Add beef chunks and sear until browned on all sides, about 4-5 minutes per side. Transfer to the slow cooker.
3. Add sliced onion and mashed garlic in the same skillet, and sauté for 2-3 minutes until softened. Place them in the slow cooker on top of the beef.
4. Arrange the carrots, potatoes, and celery around and on top of the beef in the slow cooker.
5. Mix the beef broth, Worcestershire sauce, rosemary, and thyme in a small bowl. Drizzle the mixture over the meat chunks and vegetables in the slow cooker.
6. Cover and cook on low for 8 hours or until the beef is tender.
7. Carefully remove the beef from a serving dish and arrange the vegetables around it. Skim any fat from the juices left in the slow cooker and serve as a gravy over the roast and vegetables.

Nutritional Values (per serving):

Calories: 510, Protein: 44g, Carbohydrate: 37g, Fat: 22g

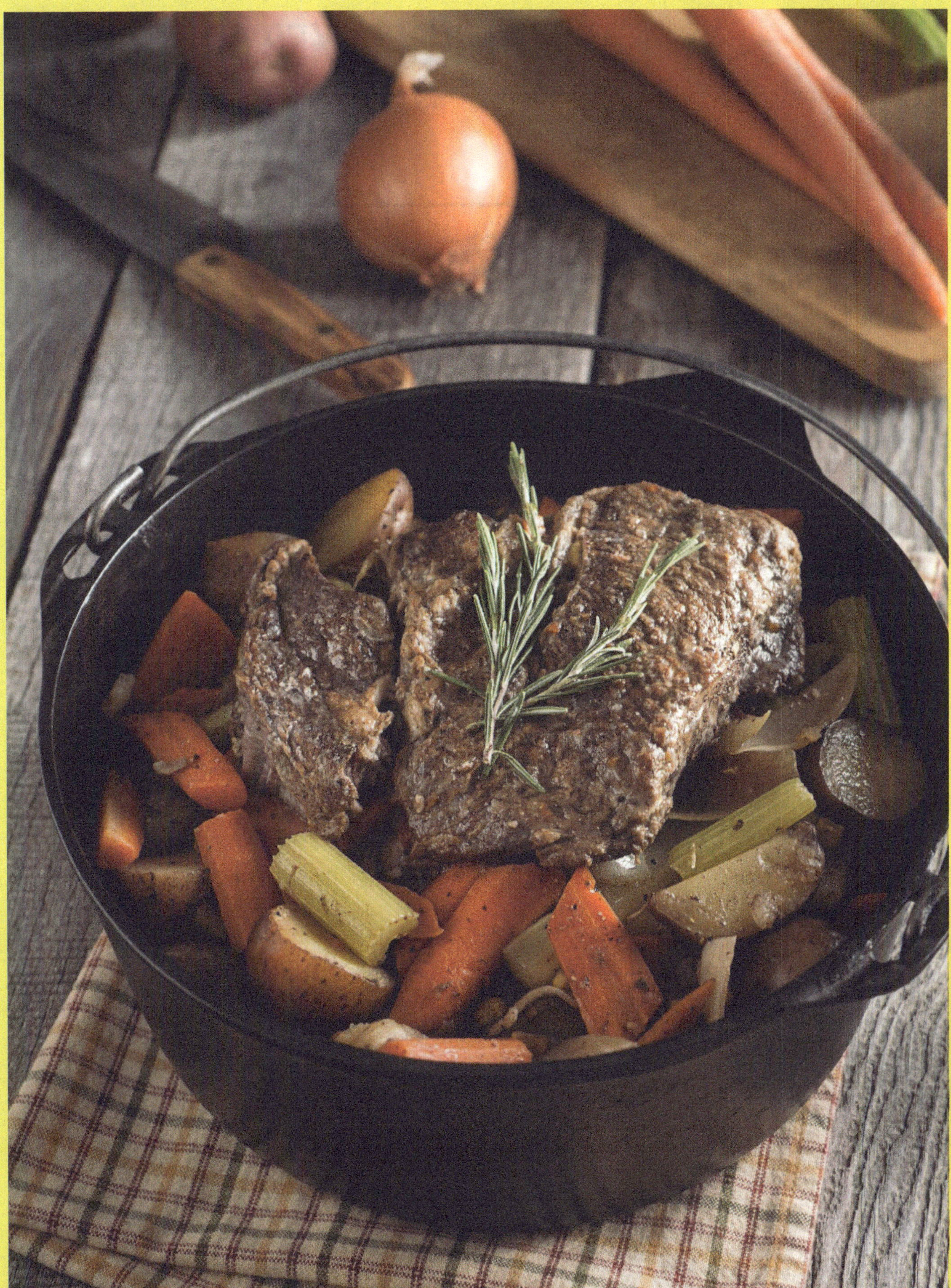

SLOW COOKER CHICKEN FAJITAS

INGREDIENTS

- 1.5 lb. boneless, skinless chicken breasts
- 1 red bell pepper, sliced
- 1 yellow bell pepper, sliced
- 1 green bell pepper, sliced
- 1 onion, sliced
- 2 cloves garlic, minced
- 1 tablespoon chili powder
- 2 teaspoons cumin
- 1 teaspoon paprika
- 1 teaspoon salt
- 1/2 teaspoon ground black pepper
- 1/4 cup chicken broth
- Juice of 1 lime
- 8 flour tortillas, warmed

Prep Time: 15 mins **Cook Time: 4 hours** **Serving: 4**

INSTRUCTIONS

1. Place chicken breasts in the slow cooker. Top with bell peppers and onion.
2. Mix the garlic, chili powder, cumin, paprika, salt, and black pepper in a small bowl. Sprinkle the seasoning mix over meat and vegetables.
3. Pour the chicken broth around the slow cooker edges.
4. Cover and cook on low for 4 hours or until the chicken is cooked through and tender.
5. Remove the chicken and shred it, then put the shredded chicken back and add lime juice. Stir to combine.
6. Serve the chicken and vegetable mixture on warmed flour tortillas and your favorite fajita toppings.

Nutritional Values (per serving):

Calories: 390, Protein: 36g, Carbohydrate: 38g, Fat: 9g

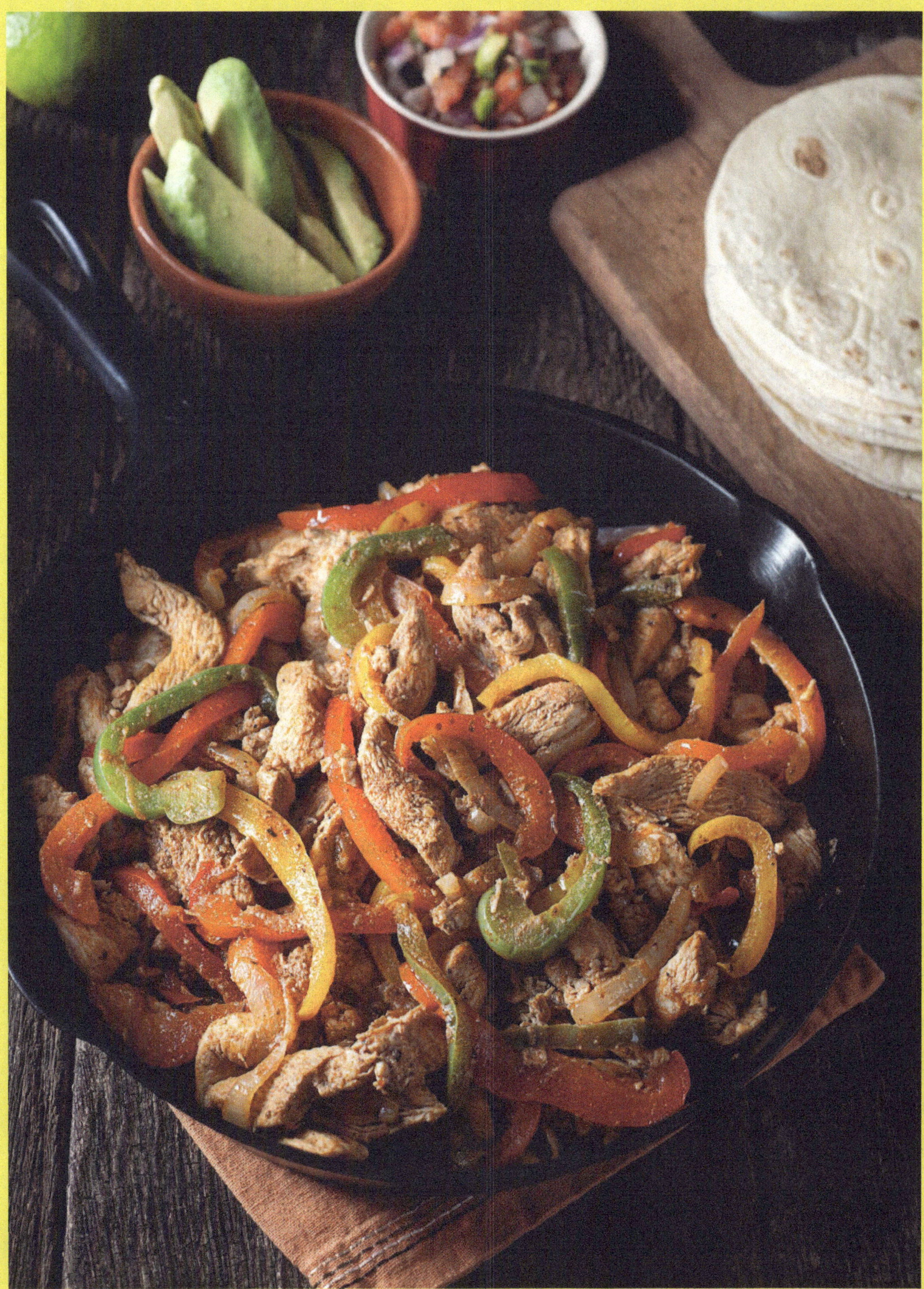

CROCKPOT BBQ RIBS

Prep Time: 10 mins **Cook Time:** 8 hours **Serving:** 4

INGREDIENTS

- 2 lbs pork ribs
- 1 teaspoon salt
- 1/2 teaspoon ground black pepper
- 1/2 teaspoon garlic powder
- 1/2 teaspoon onion powder
- 1 cup BBQ sauce

INSTRUCTIONS

1. Powder the pork ribs with salt, crushed pepper, garlic powder, and onion powder.
2. Place the ribs in the slow cooker, curling them around the edge if needed.
3. Pour the barbecue sauce over the ribs, ensuring they are well coated.
4. Cover and cook on low for 8 hours or until the ribs are tender and the meat easily separates from the bone.
5. Carefully remove the ribs and arrange them on a baking sheet. Brush with additional barbecue sauce if desired.
6. Broil in the oven for 3-5 minutes or until the sauce is caramelized and bubbly.
7. Serve hot with more BBQ sauce on the side.

Nutritional Values (per serving):

Calories: 480, Protein: 24g, Carbohydrate: 35g, Fat: 27

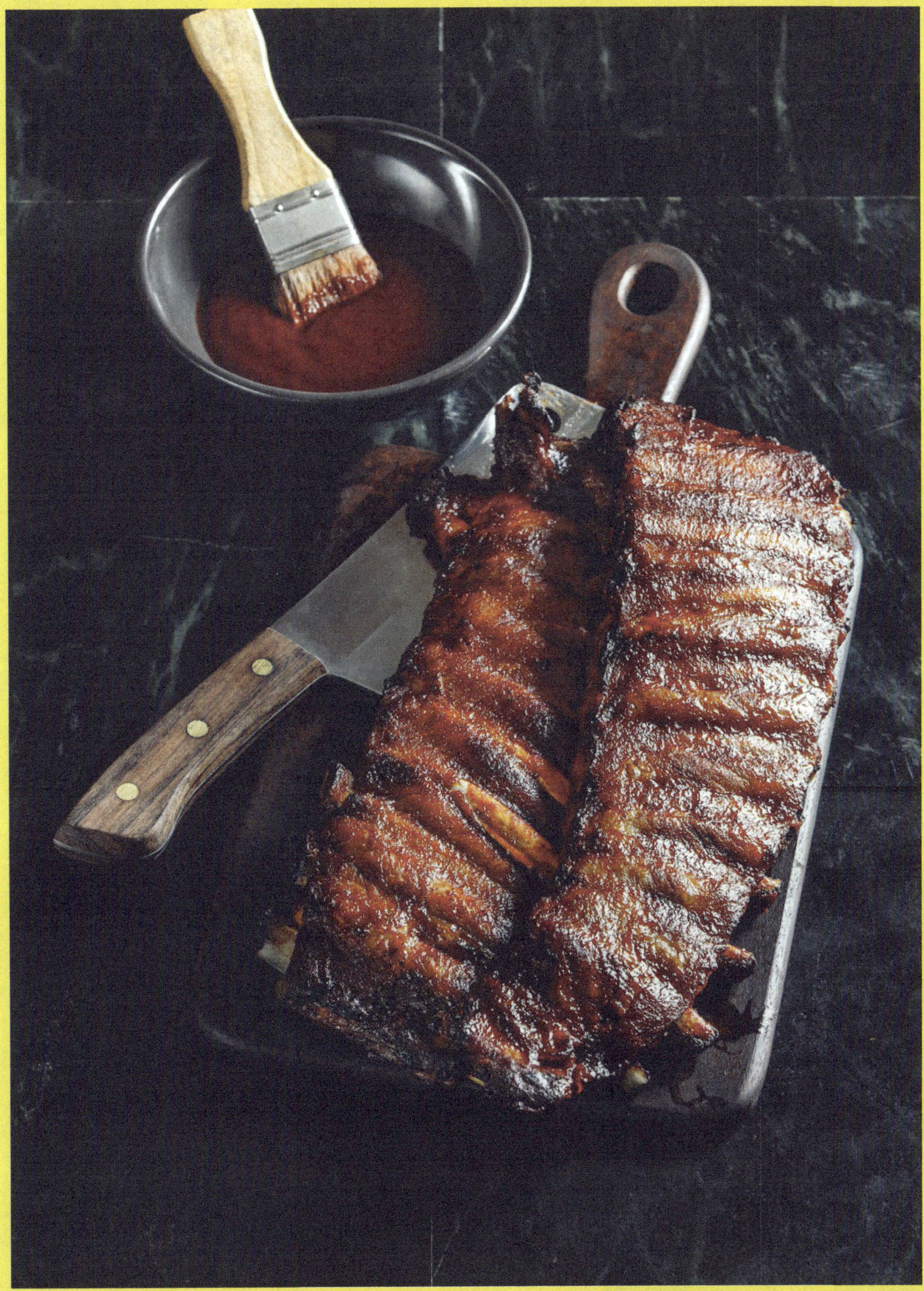

VEGETABLE SOUP

Prep Time: 15 mins   **Cook Time: 6 hours**   **Serving: 6**

INGREDIENTS

- 1 tablespoon olive oil
- 1 onion, diced
- 1 cup trimmed green beans, chopped
- 2 carrots, peeled and sliced
- 2 stalks celery, sliced
- 3 cloves garlic, minced
- 1 bell pepper, diced
- 1 can (14.5 oz) diced tomatoes, undrained
- 4 cups vegetable broth
- 1 zucchini, diced
- 1 teaspoon dried oregano
- 1 teaspoon dried basil
- Salt and pepper to taste
- 1 cup frozen peas
- 1 cup frozen corn

INSTRUCTIONS

1. Heat one tbsp oil in a skillet over medium heat. Add onion, carrots, celery, and sauté until softened, about 5 minutes. Add garlic and sauté for another minute. Transfer to the slow cooker.
2. Add zucchini, green beans, bell pepper, diced tomatoes (with juice), vegetable broth, oregano, and basil to the slow cooker. Season with salt and pepper to taste.
3. Cover and cook on low for 6 hours. Stir in frozen peas and corn in the last 30 minutes of cooking.
4. Adjust seasoning if necessary before serving.

Nutritional Values (per serving):

Calories: 120, Protein: 4g, Carbohydrate: 24g, Fat: 2g

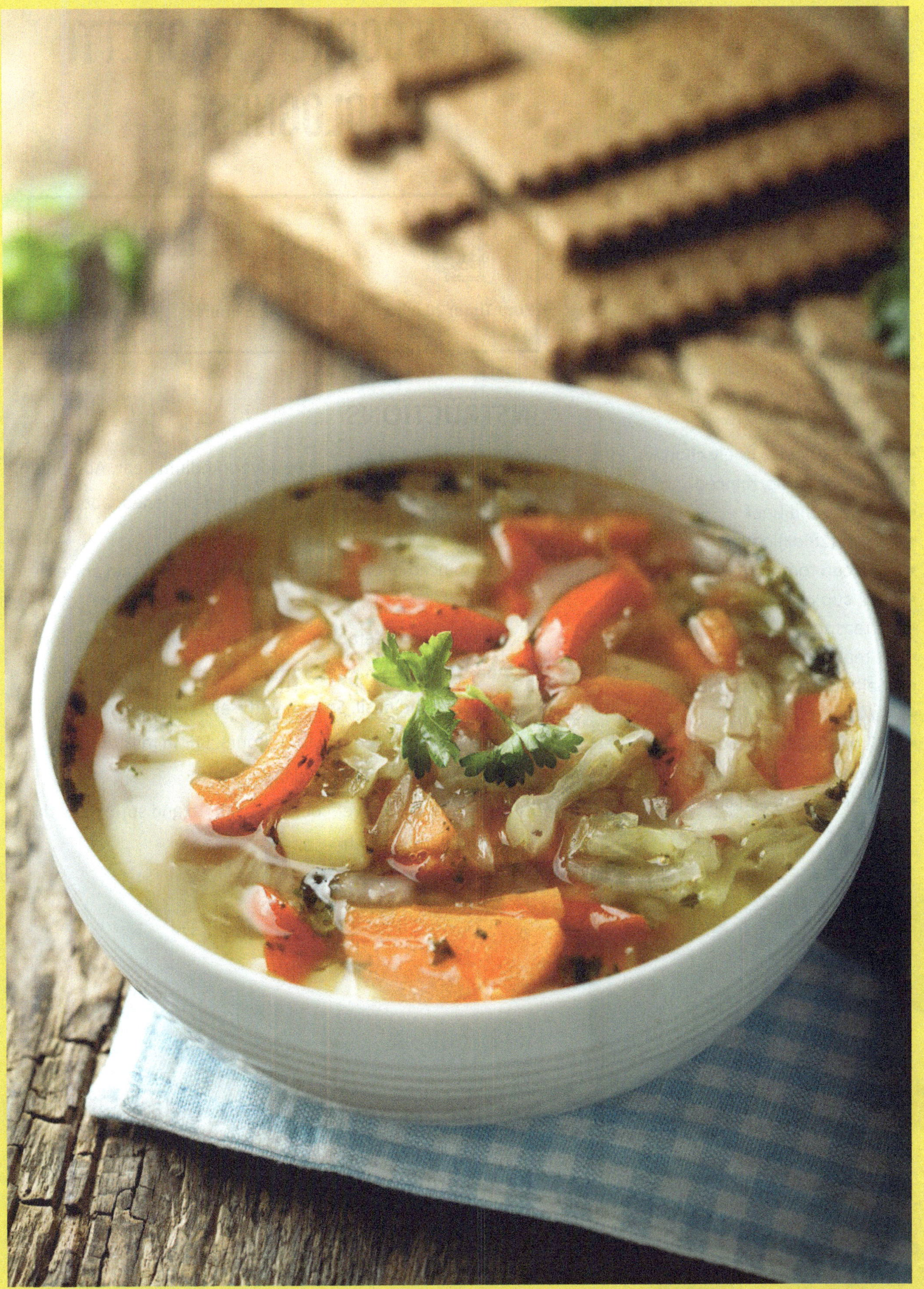

SLOW COOKER SPAGHETTI BOLOGNESE

Prep Time: 20 mins **Cook Time: 6 hours** **Serving: 6**

INGREDIENTS

- 1 tablespoon olive oil
- 1 onion, finely chopped
- 2 carrots, peeled and finely chopped
- 2 celery stalks, finely chopped
- 3 cloves garlic, minced
- 1 lb ground beef
- 1 can (28 oz) crushed tomatoes
- 1/4 cup tomato paste
- 1/2 cup red wine (optional)
- 1 teaspoon dried oregano
- 1 teaspoon dried basil
- Salt and pepper to taste
- 1/4 cup milk
- 12 oz spaghetti, cooked and drained
- Grated Parmesan cheese for serving

INSTRUCTIONS

1. Heat one tbsp oil in a skillet over medium heat. Add onion, carrots, celery, garlic, and sauté until softened, about 5 minutes.
2. Add minced beef and cook until browned. Drain any excess fat.
3. Transfer the vegetable and beef mixture to the slow cooker. Add crushed tomatoes, tomato paste, red wine (if using), oregano, and basil. Season with salt and pepper.
4. Cover and cook on low for 6 hours. Stir in milk during the last thirty minutes of cooking.
5. Serve the sauce over cooked spaghetti and sprinkle with grated Parmesan cheese.

Nutritional Values (per serving):

Calories: 510, Protein: 27g, Carbohydrate: 65g, Fat: 16g

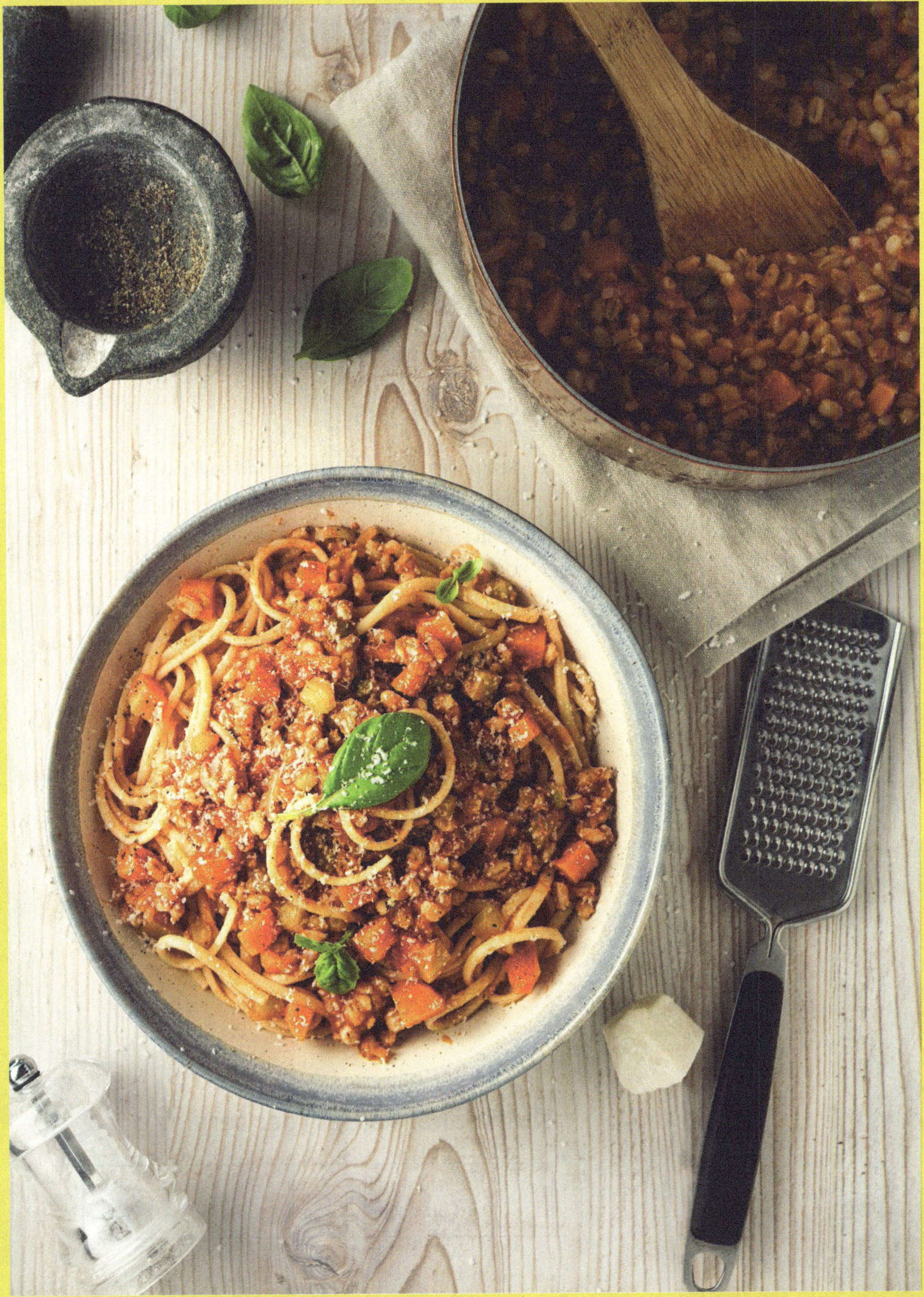

MOROCCAN LAMB TAGINE

Prep Time: 20 mins   **Cook Time:** 8 hours   **Serving:** 6

INGREDIENTS

- 2 lbs lamb shoulder, cut into 1 1/2-inch pieces
- 1 teaspoon salt
- 1/2 teaspoon ground black pepper
- 2 tablespoons olive oil
- 1 large onion, chopped
- 3 cloves garlic, minced
- 1 teaspoon ground cumin
- 1 teaspoon ground cinnamon
- 1/2 teaspoon ground ginger
- 1/4 teaspoon ground turmeric
- 1/4 teaspoon cayenne pepper
- 1 can (14.5 oz) diced tomatoes
- 1 cup chicken or beef broth
- 1 tablespoon honey
- 1 cup dried apricots, chopped
- 1/2 cup sliced almonds, toasted
- Fresh cilantro, chopped, for garnish

INSTRUCTIONS

1. Season lamb pieces with salt and pepper.
2. Heat two tbsp oil in a skillet over medium-high heat. Add lamb and brown on all sides. Transfer to the slow cooker.
3. Use the same skillet to soften the onion and mashed garlic. Add cumin, cinnamon, ginger, turmeric, and cayenne pepper, cooking for another minute. Transfer to the slow cooker.
4. Add diced tomatoes (with juice), broth, and honey to the slow cooker. Stir to combine.
5. Cover and cook on low for 8 hours or until the lamb is tender. Stir in dried apricots during the last hour of cooking.
6. Serve garnished with toasted almonds and fresh cilantro.

Nutritional Values (per serving):

Calories: 400, Protein: 28g, Carbohydrate: 35g, Fat: 18g

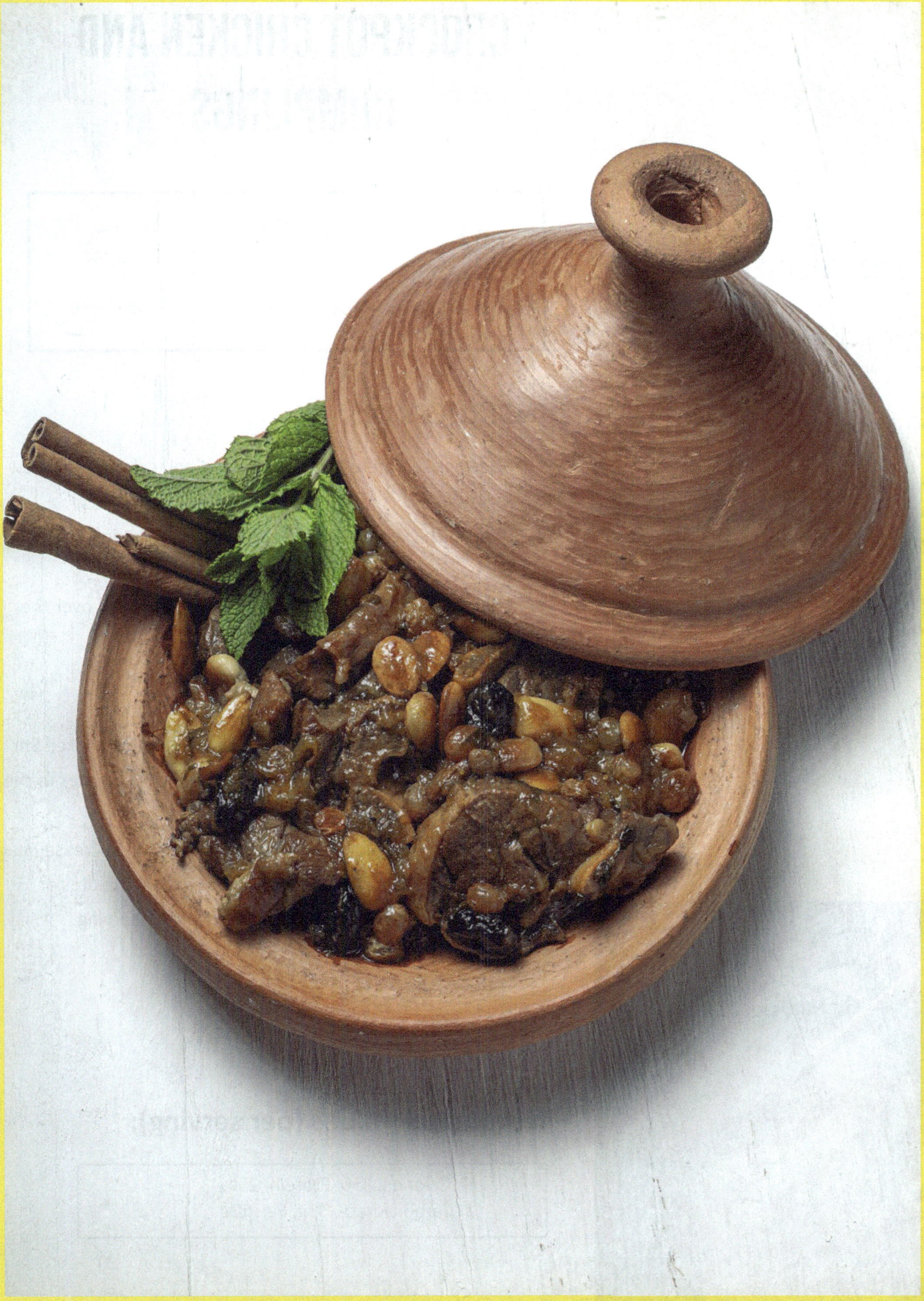

CROCKPOT CHICKEN AND DUMPLINGS

INGREDIENTS

- 1 lb chicken breasts
- 1 onion, chopped
- 2 carrots, sliced
- 2 celery stalks, sliced
- 4 cups chicken broth
- 1 teaspoon poultry seasoning
- Salt and pepper to taste
- 1 can (10.5 oz weight) cream of chicken soup
- 1 cup frozen peas
- 1 can (7.5 oz) refrigerated biscuit dough torn into pieces

Prep Time: 15 mins **Cook Time:** 6 hours **Serving:** 6

INSTRUCTIONS

1. Place chicken breasts, onion, carrots, and celery in the slow cooker.
2. Ladle in chicken broth, and add poultry seasoning, salt, and pepper. Stir to combine.
3. Do not stir; just spoon the cream of chicken soup over the top.
4. Once the chicken is cooked, cook it on low for five to six hours with a cover on.
5. Shred the chicken after taking it out of the slow cooker. Stir in the frozen peas and put the shredded chicken back to the slow cooker.
6. Spread torn biscuit dough pieces over the top. Increase heat to high, cover, and cook for another 60 to 90 minutes or until the dough is cooked. Stir gently before serving.

Nutritional Values (per serving):

Calories: 350, Protein: 25g, Carbohydrate: 33g, Fat: 12g

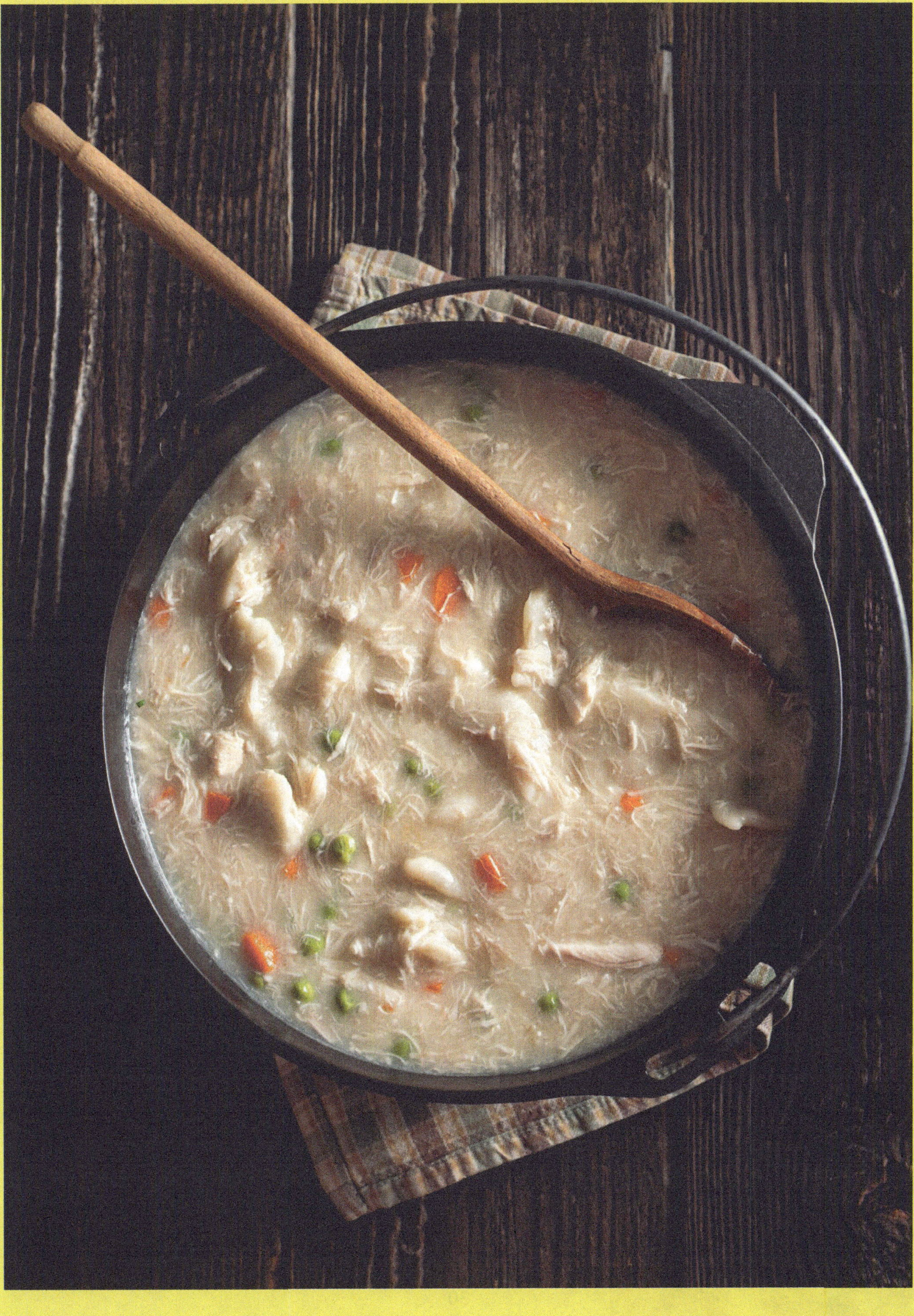

MEXICAN SHREDDED BEEF FOR TACOS

Prep Time: 15 mins **Cook Time:** 8 hours **Serving:** 6

INGREDIENTS

- 2 lbs beef chuck roast
- 1 teaspoon salt
- 1/2 teaspoon black pepper
- 1 tablespoon chili powder
- 2 teaspoons cumin
- 1 teaspoon garlic powder
- 1 onion, sliced
- 2 cloves garlic, minced
- 1 can (4 oz) diced green chilies
- 1/2 cup beef broth

INSTRUCTIONS

1. Rub the beef chuck roast with salt, pepper, chili powder, cumin, and garlic powder.
2. Place the seasoned chunk of meat in the slow cooker. Top with sliced onion, minced garlic, and diced green chilies.
3. Pour beef broth around the beef.
4. Cover and cook on low for 8 hours or until the beef is tender and shreds quickly with a fork.
5. Shred the beef and stir to mix with the cooking juices.
6. Serve the shredded beef in tacos with your favorite toppings.

Nutritional Values (per serving):

Calories: 330, Protein: 35g, Carbohydrate: 5g, Fat: 18g

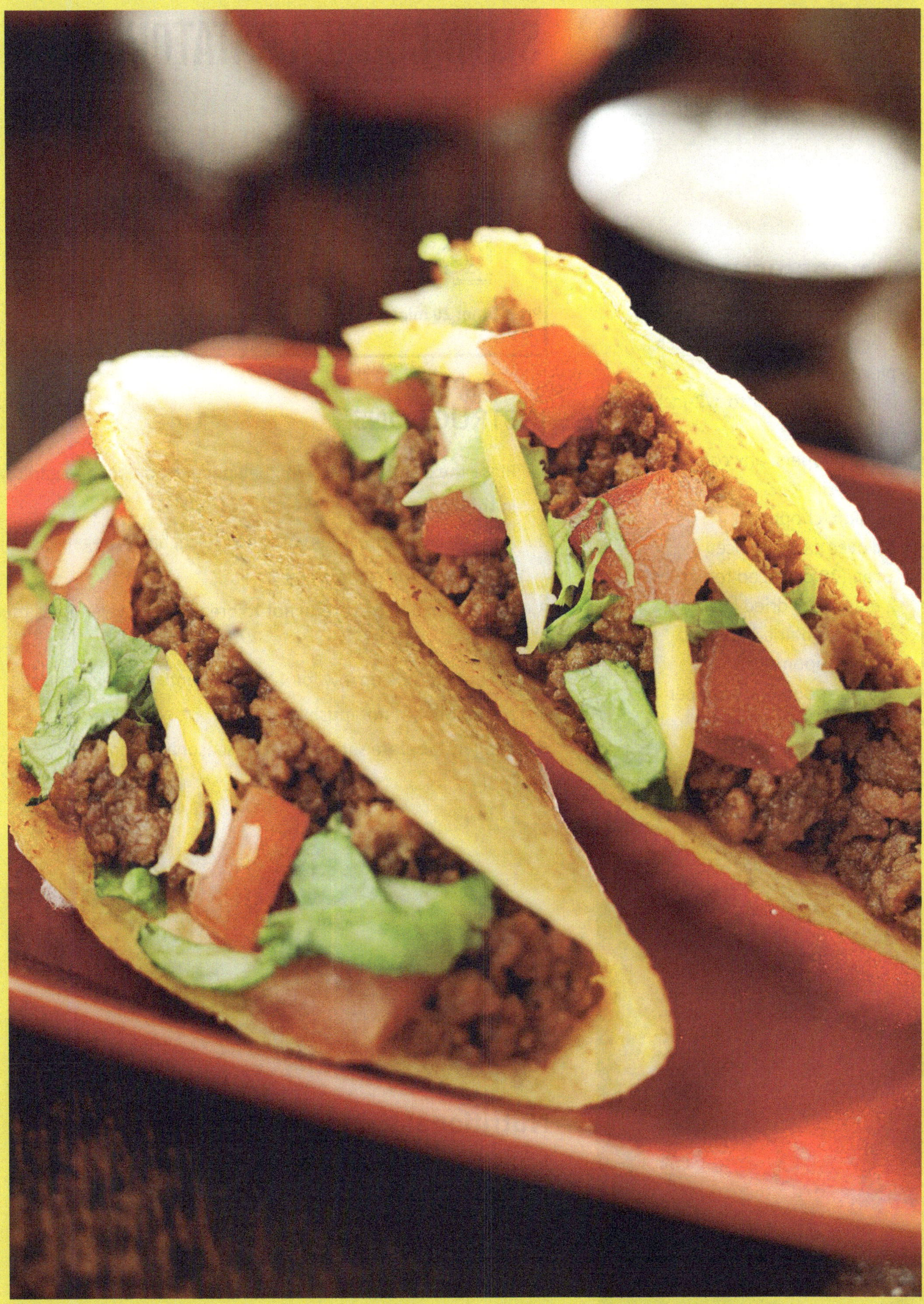

SLOW COOKER RATATOUILLE

Prep Time: 20 mins   **Cook Time:** 4 hours   **Serving:** 6

INGREDIENTS

- 1 eggplant, cut into 1/2-inch pieces
- 2 zucchinis, cut into 1/2-inch pieces
- 2 bell peppers, any color, chopped
- 1 onion, chopped
- 3 cloves garlic, minced
- 1 can (28 oz) diced tomatoes
- 2 teaspoons dried basil
- 1 teaspoon dried oregano
- 1/2 teaspoon salt
- 1/4 teaspoon black pepper
- 2 tablespoons olive oil

INSTRUCTIONS

1. Place the eggplant, zucchini, bell peppers, onion, and garlic in the slow cooker.
2. Add the diced tomatoes with their juice, basil, oregano, salt, and pepper. Drizzle with olive oil.
3. Gently stir, and be careful not to break up the vegetables too much.
4. Cover and cook on low for 4 hours or until the vegetables are tender but not mushy.
5. Stir gently before serving. Adjust seasoning if necessary.

Nutritional Values (per serving):

Calories: 120, Protein: 3g, Carbohydrate: 20g, Fat: 4g

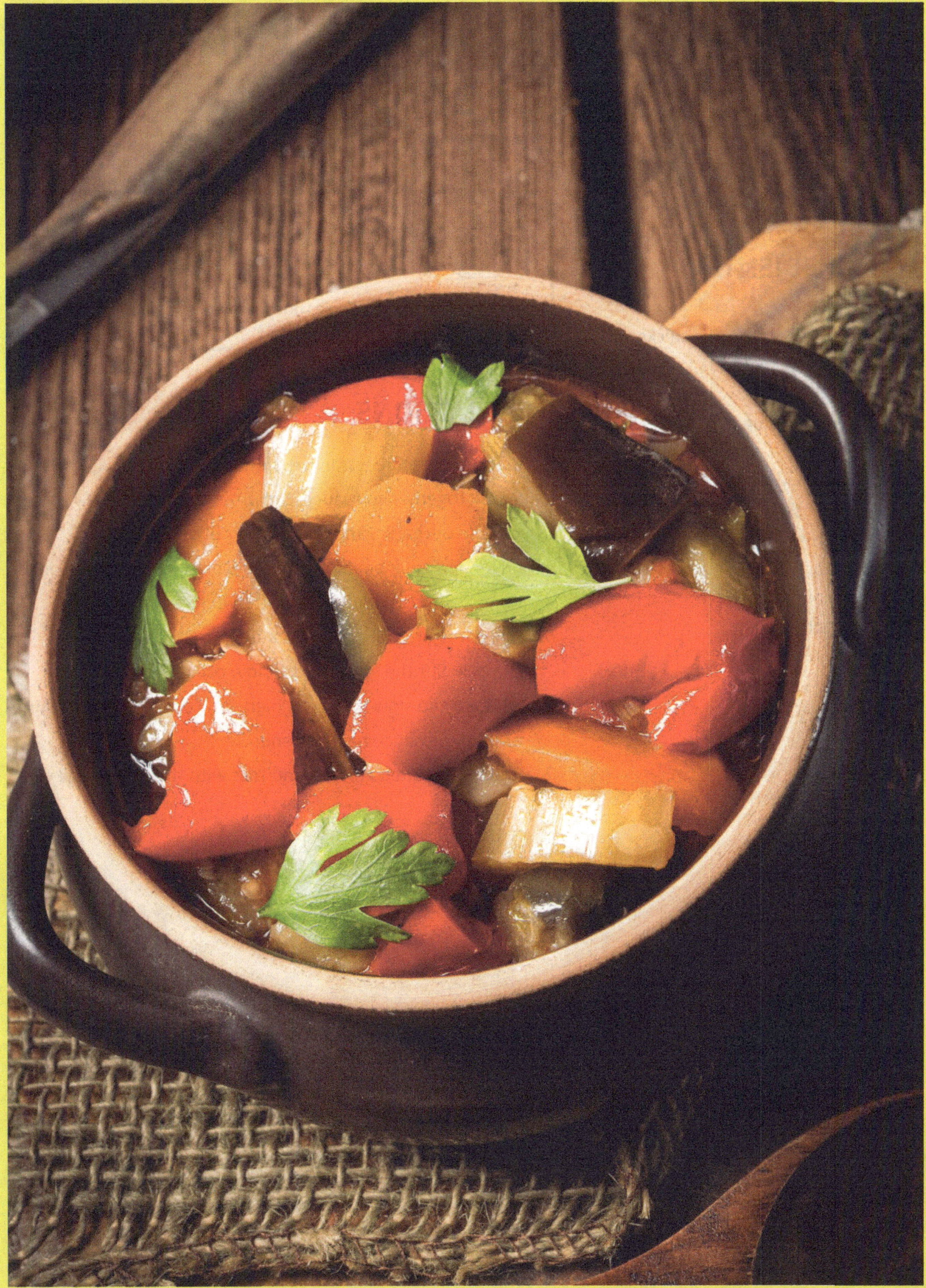

TERIYAKI CHICKEN

Prep Time: 15 mins **Cook Time: 4 hours** **Serving: 4**

INGREDIENTS

- 1.5 lb. boneless, skinless chicken breasts
- 1/2 cup soy sauce
- 1/3 cup brown sugar
- 1/4 cup water
- 2 tablespoons rice vinegar
- 1 teaspoon sesame oil
- 2 garlic cloves, minced
- 1 tablespoon fresh ginger, grated
- 1 tablespoon cornstarch
- 1 tablespoon water

INSTRUCTIONS

1. Place chicken breasts in the slow cooker.
2. Whisk together soy sauce, brown sugar, water, rice vinegar, sesame oil, garlic, and ginger. Pour over the chicken.
3. Cover and cook on low for 4 hours or until chicken is cooked.
4. Remove chicken and shred with two forks. Set aside.
5. Mix cornstarch and water in a deep-bottom bowl until smooth. Stir the sauce in the slow cooker.
6. Increase the slow cooker to high and cook for 15-20 minutes or until the sauce has thickened.
7. Return shredded chicken and toss with the sauce until well coated.

Nutritional Values (per serving):

Calories: 310, Protein: 36g, Carbohydrate: 23g, Fat: 6g

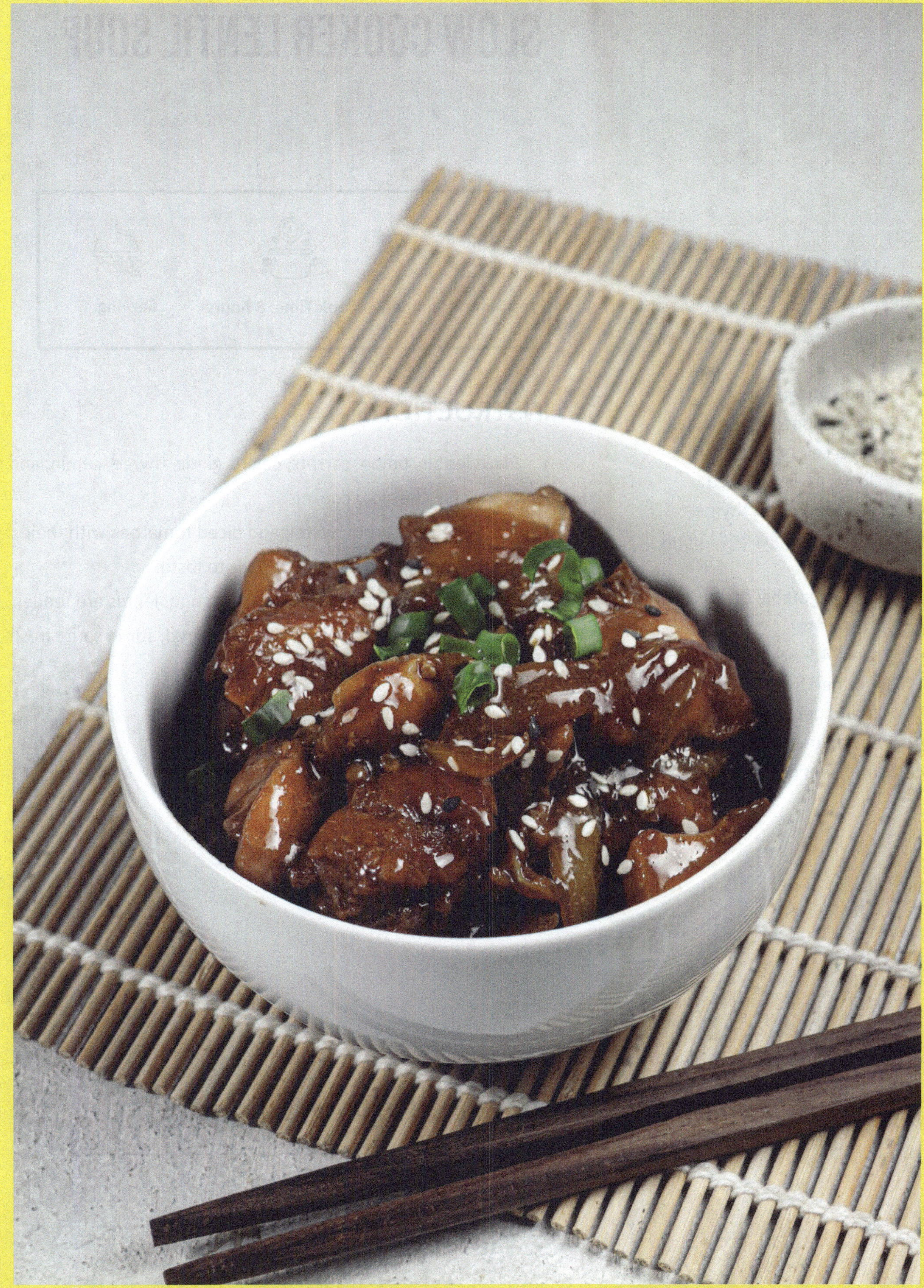

SLOW COOKER LENTIL SOUP

Prep Time: 15 mins **Cook Time: 8 hours** **Serving: 6**

INGREDIENTS

- 1 cup dried lentils, rinsed and drained
- 1 onion, diced
- 2 carrots, peeled and diced
- 2 stalks celery, diced
- 3 cloves garlic, minced
- 1 teaspoon dried thyme
- 1/2 teaspoon ground cumin
- 1 bay leaf
- 4 cups vegetable broth
- 2 cups water
- 1 can (14.5 oz) diced tomatoes, undrained
- Salt and pepper to taste
- Spinach leaves, optional
- Lemon wedges for serving

INSTRUCTIONS

1. Place lentils, onion, carrots, celery, garlic, thyme, cumin, and bay leaf in the slow cooker.
2. Add vegetable broth, water, and diced tomatoes with their juice. Season with salt and pepper to taste.
3. Cover and cook on low for 8 hours or until lentils are tender.
4. Remove bay leaf before serving. If desired, stir in some fresh spinach leaves until wilted.
5. Serve with lemon wedges on the side.

Nutritional Values (per serving):

Calories: 180, Protein: 11g, Carbohydrate: 30g, Fat: 1g

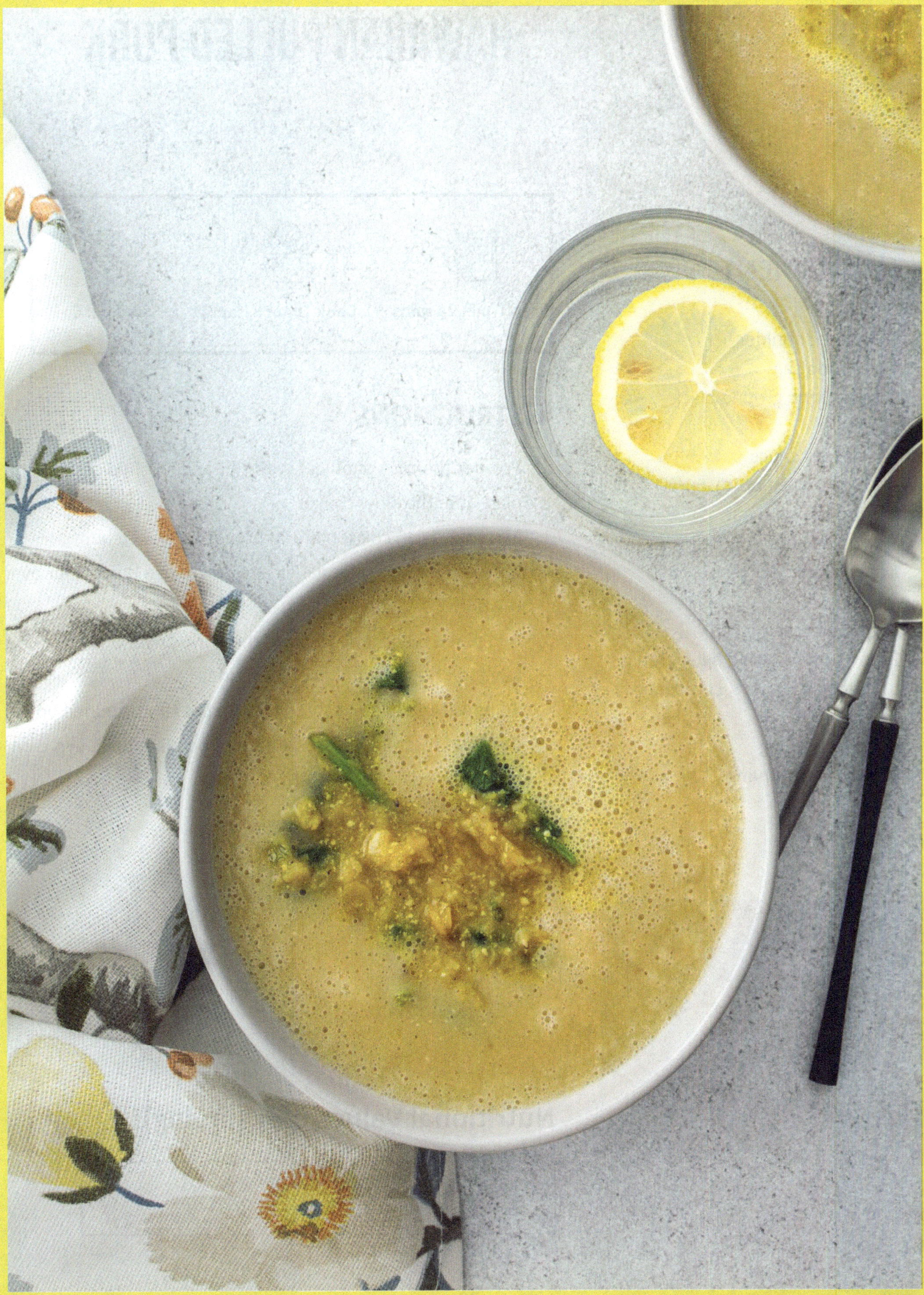

HAWAIIAN PULLED PORK

Prep Time: 20 mins | **Cook Time: 8 hours** | **Serving: 6**

INGREDIENTS

- 3 lbs pork shoulder
- 1 teaspoon salt
- 1/2 teaspoon ground black pepper
- 1/2 cup soy sauce
- 1/2 cup chicken broth
- 1/4 cup brown sugar
- 1/4 cup ketchup
- 1 tablespoon Worcestershire sauce
- 2 garlic cloves, minced
- 1 tablespoon fresh ginger, grated
- 1 pineapple, peeled, cored, and chunked
- Buns, for serving
- Coleslaw, for serving

INSTRUCTIONS

1. Powder the pork shoulder with salt and crushed pepper and place it in the slow cooker.
2. Mix soy sauce, chicken broth, brown sugar, ketchup, Worcestershire sauce, garlic, and ginger in a bowl. Pour over the pork.
3. Add pineapple chunks around the pork. Cover and cook on low for 8 hours or until pork is tender.
4. Remove the pork and shred it, then put the shredded pork back and toss them with the sauce and pineapple. Serve on buns with coleslaw.

Nutritional Values (per serving):

Calories: 500, Protein: 44g, Carbohydrate: 35g, Fat: 20g

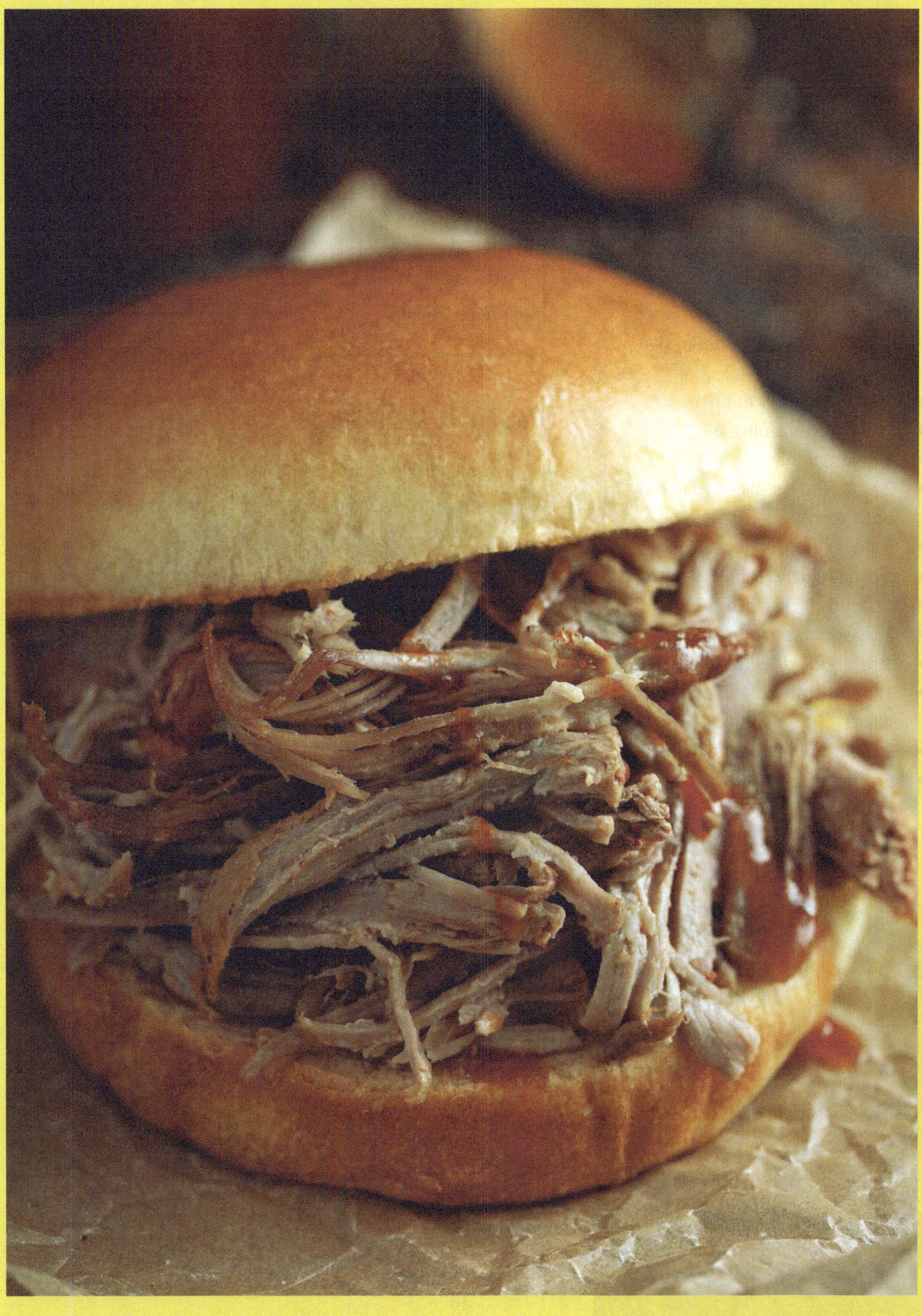

CHICKEN CACCIATORE

Prep Time: 15 mins   **Cook Time:** 6 hours   **Serving:** 4

INGREDIENTS

- 4 chicken thighs, bone-in, skin-on
- Salt and pepper to taste
- 2 tablespoons olive oil
- 1 onion, thinly sliced
- 2 bell peppers, sliced (one red, one green)
- 3 cloves garlic, minced
- 1 can (28 oz) crushed tomatoes
- 1/2 cup chicken broth
- 1 teaspoon dried oregano
- 1 teaspoon dried basil
- 1/2 cup pitted & halved black olives
- 2 tablespoons capers, drained
- Fresh parsley, chopped, for garnish

INSTRUCTIONS

1. Season chicken thighs with salt and pepper.
2. Heat two tbsp oil in a skillet over medium-high heat. Add chicken thighs, skin-side down, and sear until golden brown, about 4-5 minutes on each side. Transfer to the slow cooker.
3. In the same skillet, saute the onion with bell peppers and garlic. Sauté until softened, about 5 minutes. Transfer to the slow cooker.
4. Add crushed tomatoes, chicken broth, oregano, and basil to the slow cooker. Stir them properly.
5. Cover and cook on low for 6 hours. Stir in black olives and capers in the last 30 minutes of cooking.
6. Serve garnished with fresh parsley.

Nutritional Values (per serving):

Calories: 340, Protein: 25g, Carbohydrate: 18g, Fat: 20g

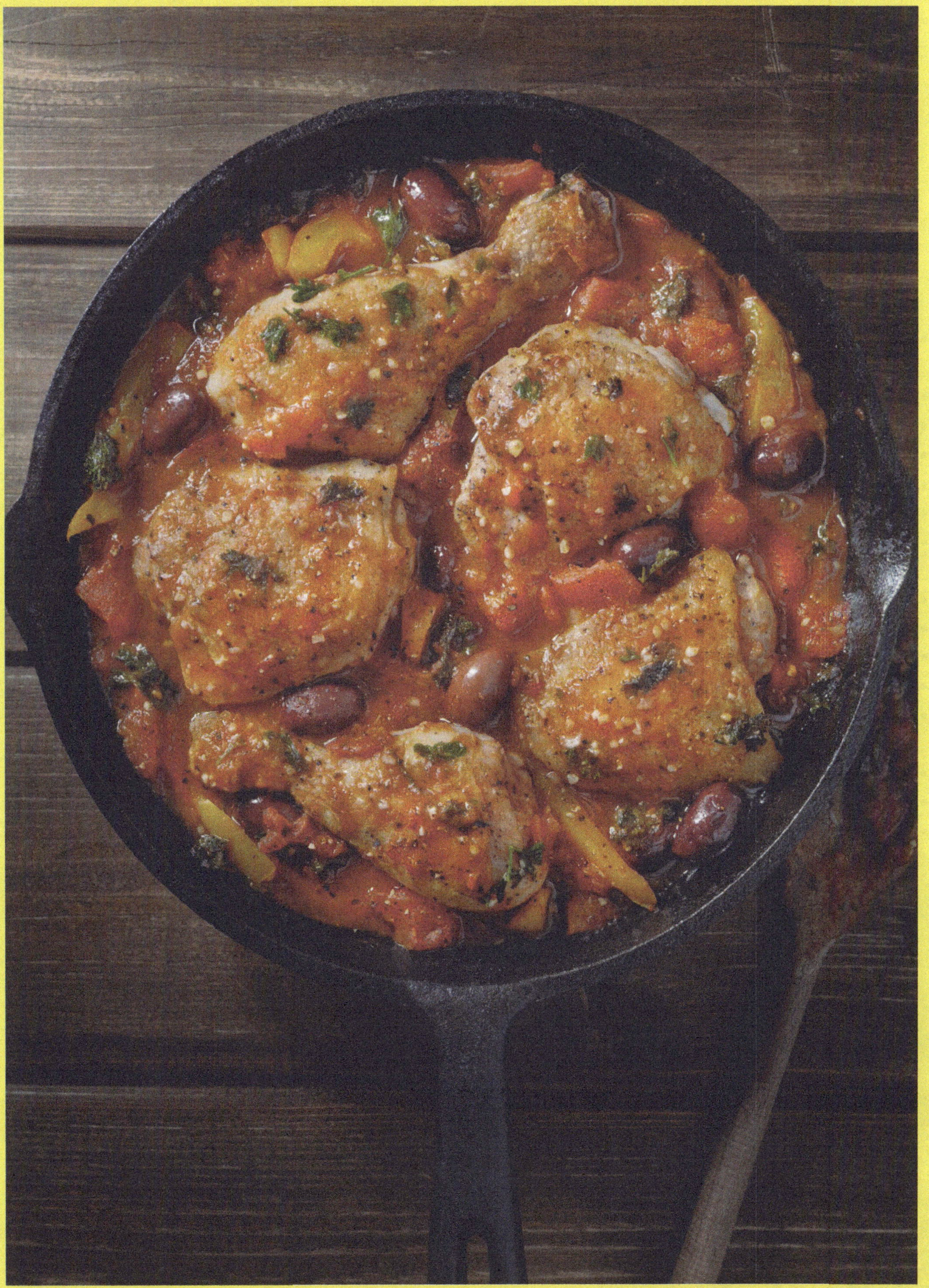

SLOW COOKER JAMBALAYA

Prep Time: 20 mins   **Cook Time:** 5 hours   **Serving:** 6

INGREDIENTS

- 1 lb chicken breast, cut into pieces
- 1 lb andouille sausage, sliced
- 1 onion, diced
- 1 green bell pepper, diced
- 2 celery stalks, diced
- 3 cloves garlic, minced
- 1 can (14.5 oz) diced tomatoes, undrained
- 1 cup chicken broth
- 2 teaspoons Cajun seasoning
- 1 teaspoon dried thyme
- 1 teaspoon dried oregano
- 1/2 lb shrimp, peeled and deveined
- 1 cup long-grain white rice
- Salt and pepper to taste
- Green onions, sliced, for garnish

INSTRUCTIONS

1. Place chicken, sausage, onion, bell pepper, celery, and garlic in the slow cooker.
2. Add diced tomatoes with their juice, chicken broth, Cajun seasoning, thyme, and oregano. Stir to combine.
3. Cover and cook on low for 4 hours. Stir in shrimp and rice, submerging the rice in the liquid. Season with salt and pepper.
4. Cover and cook more on high for one hour. Serve garnished with sliced green onions.

Nutritional Values (per serving):

Calories: 450, Protein: 35g, Carbohydrate: 38g, Fat: 18g

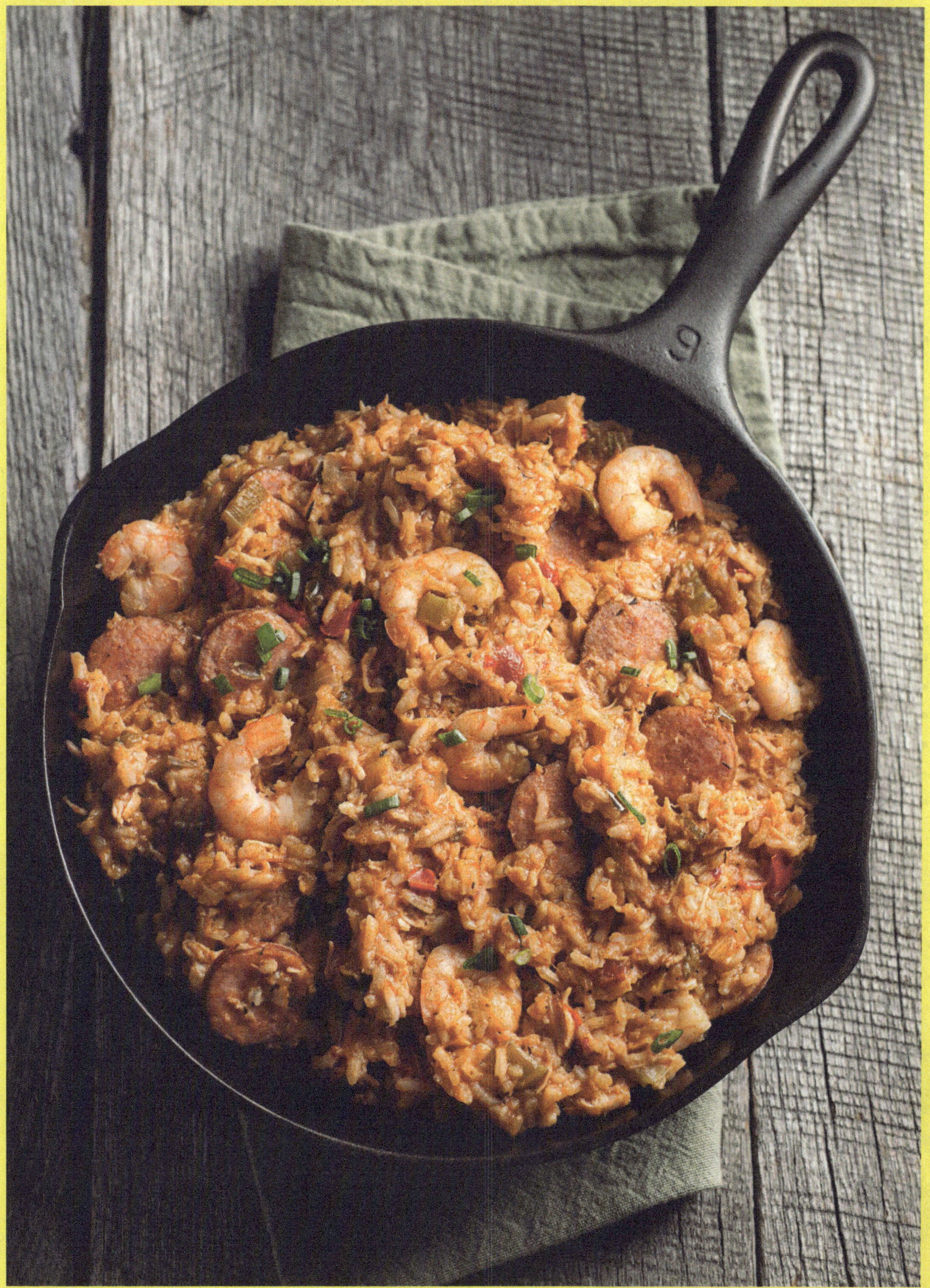

VEGETARIAN CHILI

Prep Time: 15 mins **Cook Time:** 8 hours **Serving:** 6

INGREDIENTS

- 2 cans (15 oz each weight) black beans, drained and rinsed
- 1 can (15 oz weight) kidney beans, drained and rinsed
- 1 can (15 oz weight) pinto beans, drained and rinsed
- 1 large onion, diced
- 1 green bell pepper, diced
- 2 carrots, peeled and diced
- 2 stalks celery, diced
- 3 cloves garlic, minced
- 1 can (28 oz) crushed tomatoes
- 1 cup vegetable broth
- 2 tablespoons chili powder
- 1 tablespoon cumin
- 1 teaspoon smoked paprika
- Salt and pepper to taste

INSTRUCTIONS

1. Toss the beans with onion, bell pepper, carrots, celery, garlic, crushed tomatoes, vegetable broth, chili powder, cumin, and smoked paprika in the slow cooker.
2. Stir to mix well. Powder it with salt and pepper to taste.
3. Cover and cook on low for 8 hours. Serve hot.

Nutritional Values (per serving):

Calories: 290, Protein: 16g, Carbohydrate: 54g, Fat: 2g

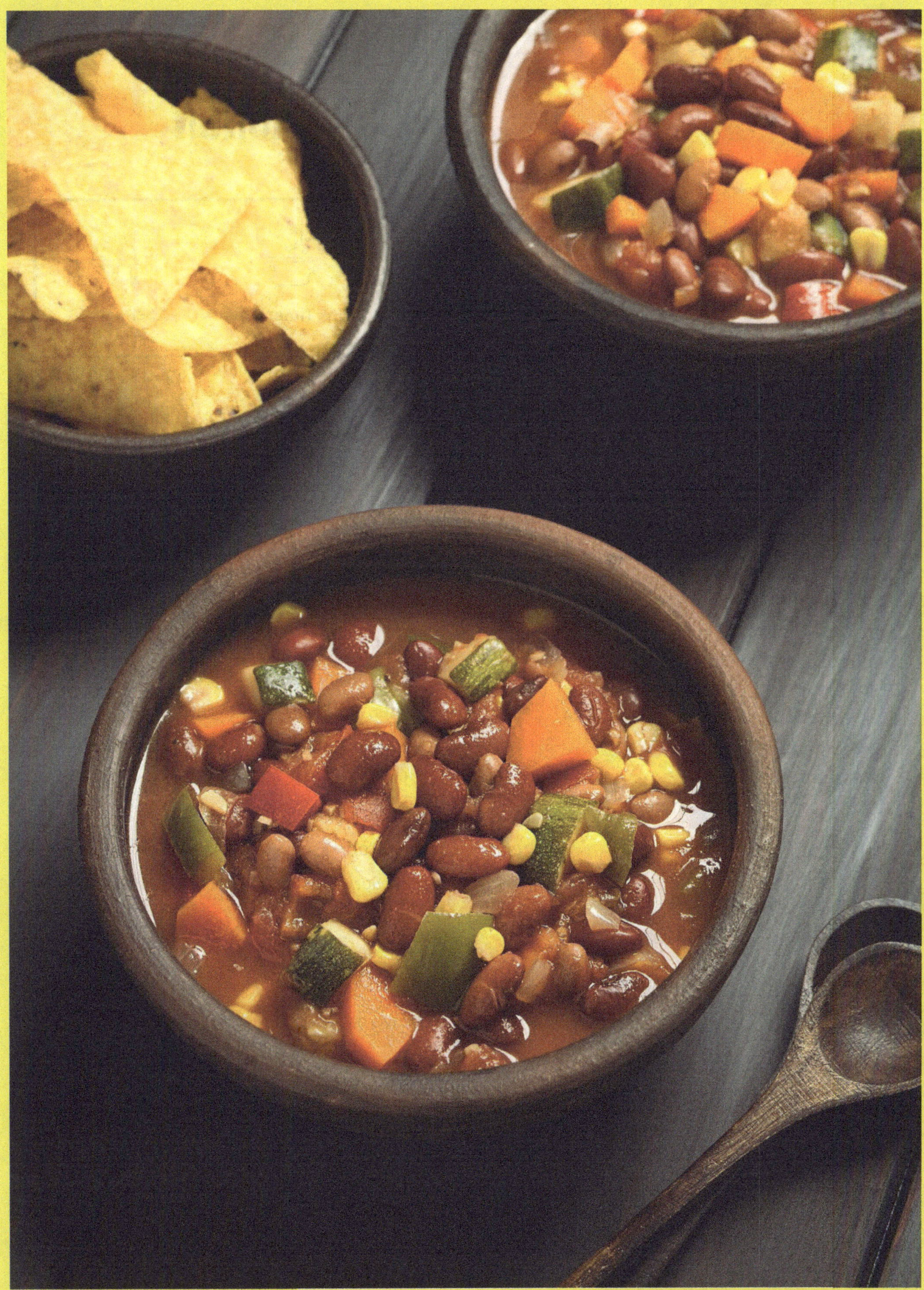

CROCKPOT BEEF BOURGUIGNON

Prep Time: 30 mins **Cook Time:** 8 hours **Serving:** 6

INGREDIENTS

- 2 lb. beef chuck, cut into 1-inch cubes
- Salt and pepper to taste
- 2 tablespoons olive oil
- 1 large onion, diced
- 2 carrots, peeled and sliced
- 2 garlic cloves, minced
- 1/2 cup brandy (optional)
- 2 cups dry red wine
- 2 cups beef broth
- 2 tablespoons tomato paste
- 1 teaspoon fresh thyme leaves
- 2 bay leaves
- 1 cup pearl onions, peeled
- 8 ounces mushrooms, quartered
- 2 tablespoons butter
- 2 tablespoons all-purpose flour

INSTRUCTIONS

1. Powder the beef cubes with salt and pepper. Heat two tbsp oil in a skillet over medium-high heat. Add beef cubes in batches, searing until browned on all sides. Transfer to the crockpot.
2. Add diced onion and carrots in the same skillet, cooking until softened. Add mashed garlic and saute for a minute. If using, Ladle in the brandy to deglaze the pan, scraping up any browned bits. Transfer the contents to the crockpot.
3. Ladle in the red wine, beef broth, and tomato paste into the crockpot. Add thyme and bay leaves. Stir to combine.
4. Cover and cook on low for 8 hours. Add and sauté pearl onions and mushrooms in butter until golden brown in the last 30 minutes. Sprinkle flour and cook for another 1-2 minutes.
5. Add mushroom slices and onions to the crockpot. Stir well and cook on high for thirty minutes or until the sauce thickens. Remove bay leaves before serving.

Nutritional Values (per serving):

Calories: 450, Protein: 35g, Carbohydrate: 15g, Fat: 20g

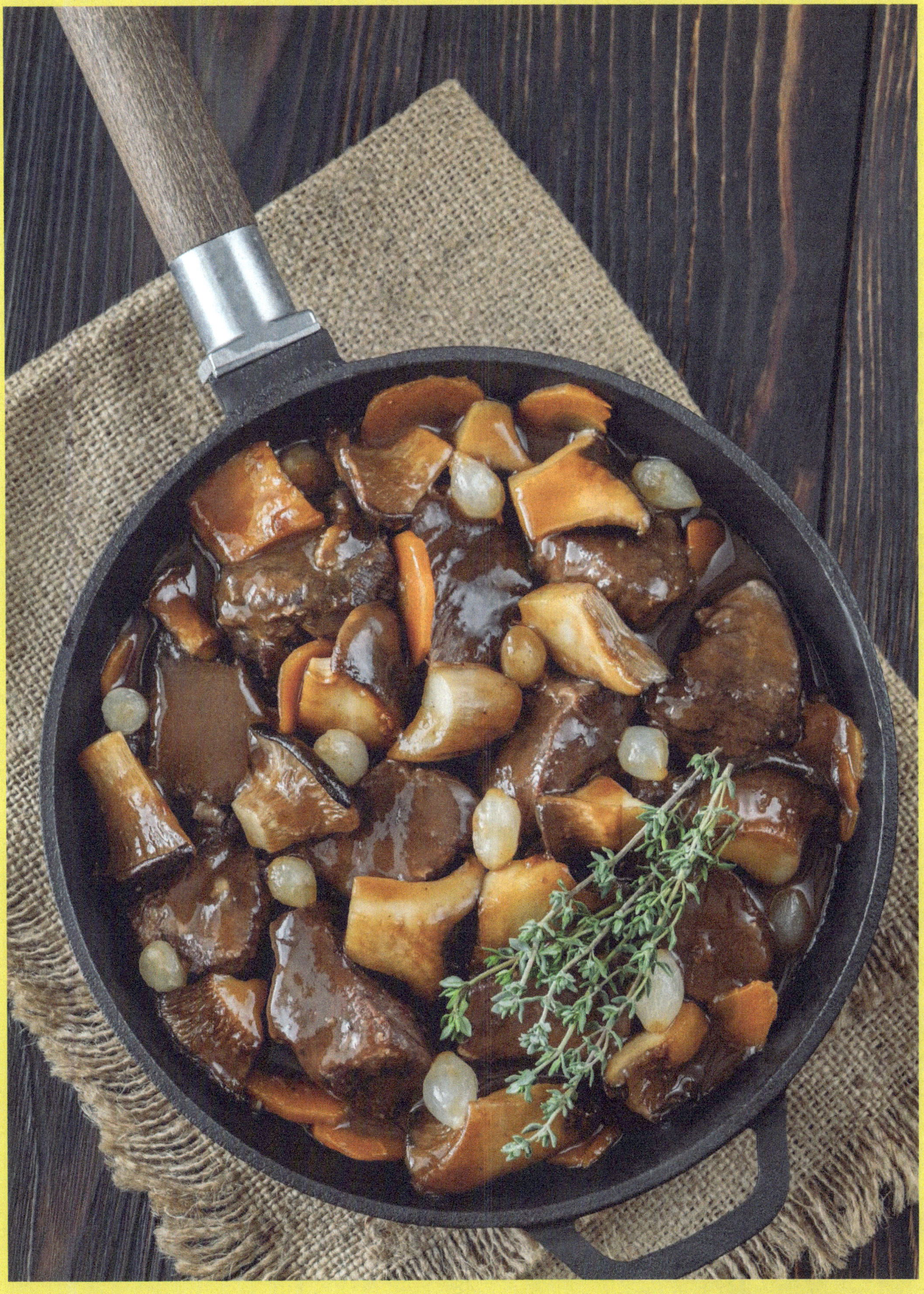

TURKEY BREAST WITH CRANBERRY SAUCE

Prep Time: 15 mins **Cook Time:** 7 hours **Serving:** 6

INGREDIENTS

- 1 turkey breast (about 3 lbs), bone-in, skin-on
- Salt and pepper to taste
- 1 onion, sliced
- 1 orange, quartered
- 1 cup cranberries (fresh or frozen)
- 1/2 cup orange juice
- 1/2 cup sugar
- 1 teaspoon dried thyme
- 1/2 teaspoon ground cinnamon

INSTRUCTIONS

1. Powder the turkey breast with salt and pepper. Place it in the crockpot.
2. Add the sliced onion and quarters of an orange around the turkey.
3. Combine the cranberries, orange juice, sugar, thyme, and cinnamon in a saucepan and cook for 7-10 minutes.
4. Pour the cranberry sauce over the turkey in the crockpot.
5. Cover and cook on low for 6-7 hours or until the turkey is cooked.
6. Rest the turkey for 8-10 minutes before slicing. Serve with the cranberry sauce.

Nutritional Values (per serving):

Calories: 350, Protein: 48g, Carbohydrate: 20g, Fat: 7g

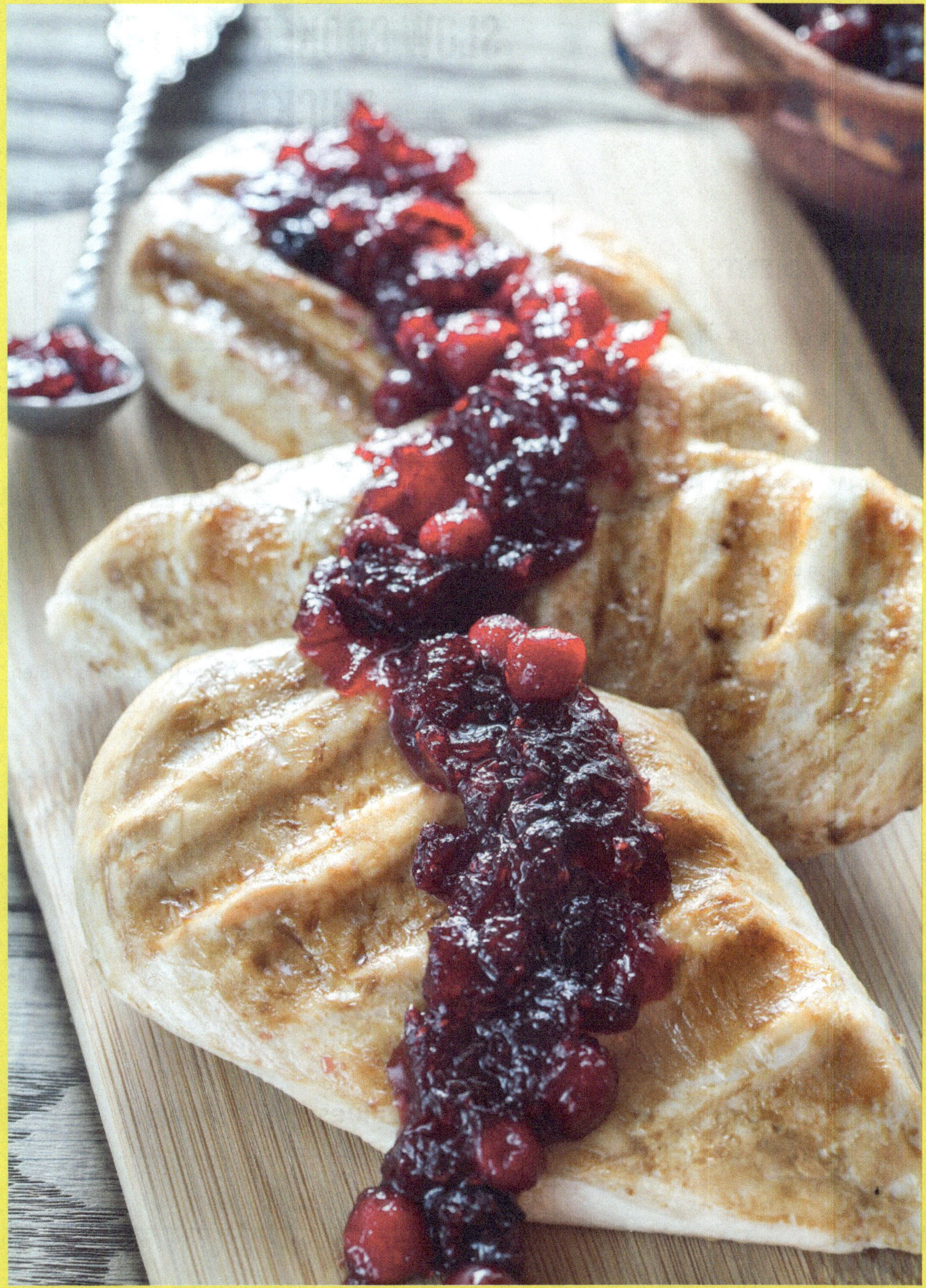

SLOW COOKER BUTTER CHICKEN

Prep Time: 15 mins **Cook Time: 4 hours** **Serving: 6**

INGREDIENTS

- 2 lb. without bone & skin chicken thighs, cut into pieces
- 1 onion, finely chopped
- 3 garlic cloves, minced
- 1 tablespoon fresh ginger, grated
- 1 can (14 oz) tomato puree
- 1 tablespoon garam masala
- 1 teaspoon chili powder
- 1 teaspoon cumin
- 1 teaspoon turmeric
- 1 cup heavy cream
- 4 tablespoons unsalted butter
- Salt to taste
- Fresh cilantro, chopped, for garnish

INSTRUCTIONS

1. Place the chicken pieces in the crockpot.
2. Add the onion, garlic, ginger, tomato puree, garam masala, chili powder, cumin, and turmeric. Stir to combine properly and coat the chicken well.
3. Cover and cook on low for 4 hours until the chicken is tender.
4. Stir in the heavy cream and butter until the butter is melted and the sauce is creamy. Powder it with salt to taste.
5. Serve garnished with chopped cilantro.

Nutritional Values (per serving):

Calories: 490, Protein: 35g, Carbohydrate: 10g, Fat: 36g

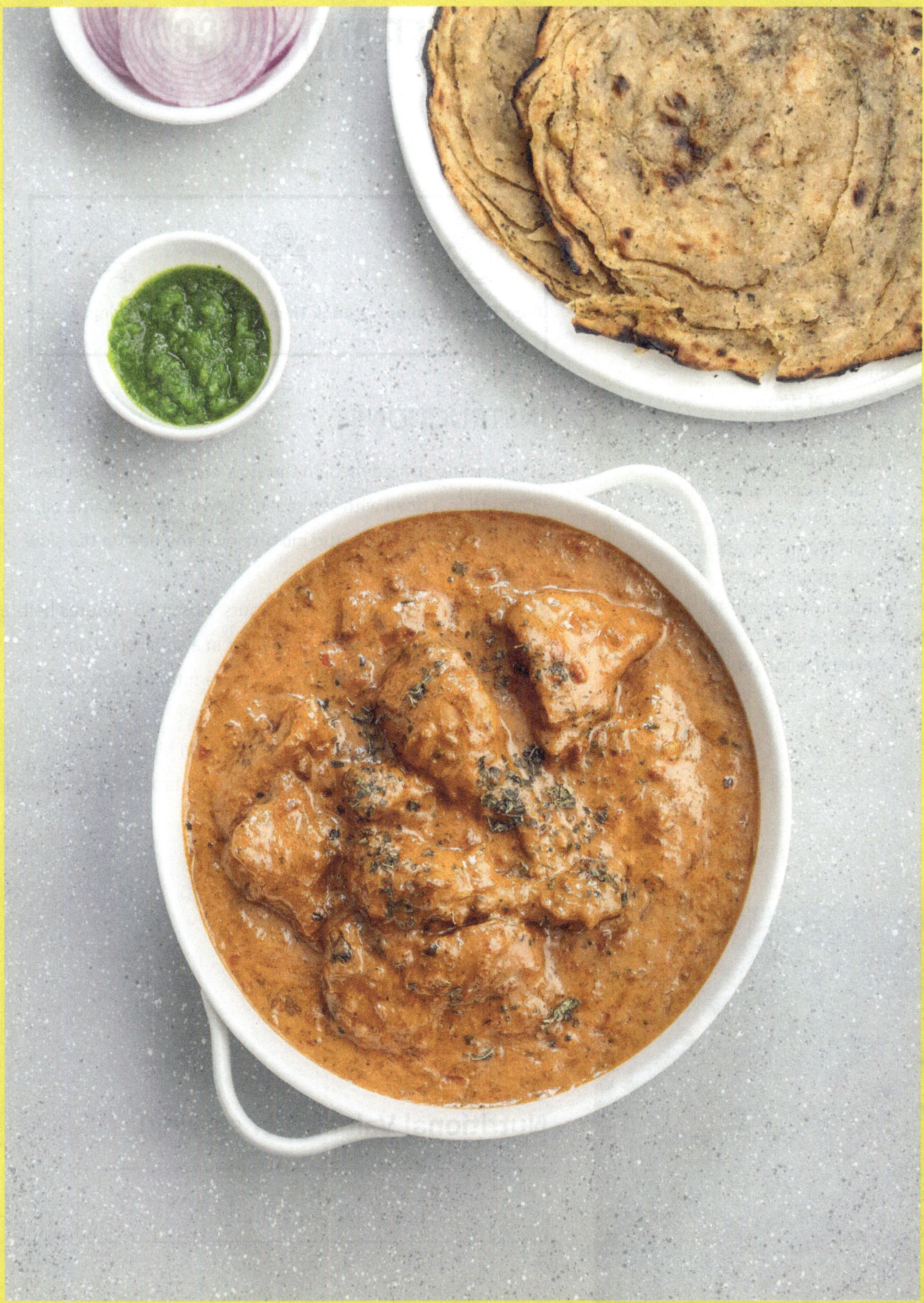

BEEF AND BROCCOLI

INGREDIENTS

- 1 1/2 lbs beef sirloin, sliced into thin strips
- 1 cup beef broth
- 1/2 cup soy sauce
- 1/3 cup brown sugar
- 1 tablespoon sesame oil
- 3 garlic cloves, minced
- 2 tablespoons cornstarch
- 2 tablespoons water
- 4 cups broccoli florets
- Sesame seeds, for garnish
- Cooked rice for serving

Prep Time: 15 mins **Cook Time:** 4 hours **Serving:** 4

INSTRUCTIONS

1. Place the striped meat in the slow cooker. Whisk the beef broth in a bowl with soy sauce, brown sugar, sesame oil, and minced garlic. Ladle the mixture over the beef in the slow cooker.
2. Cover and cook on low for 4 hours. About 30 minutes before serving, mix cornstarch and water in a small bowl until smooth. Toss the cornstarch mixture into the slow cooker to thicken the sauce.
3. Add broccoli florets, cover, and cook on high for 25-30 minutes or until tender. Serve the beef broccoli with cooked rice garnished with sesame seeds.

Nutritional Values (per serving):

Calories: 350, Protein: 40g, Carbohydrate: 25g, Fat: 10g

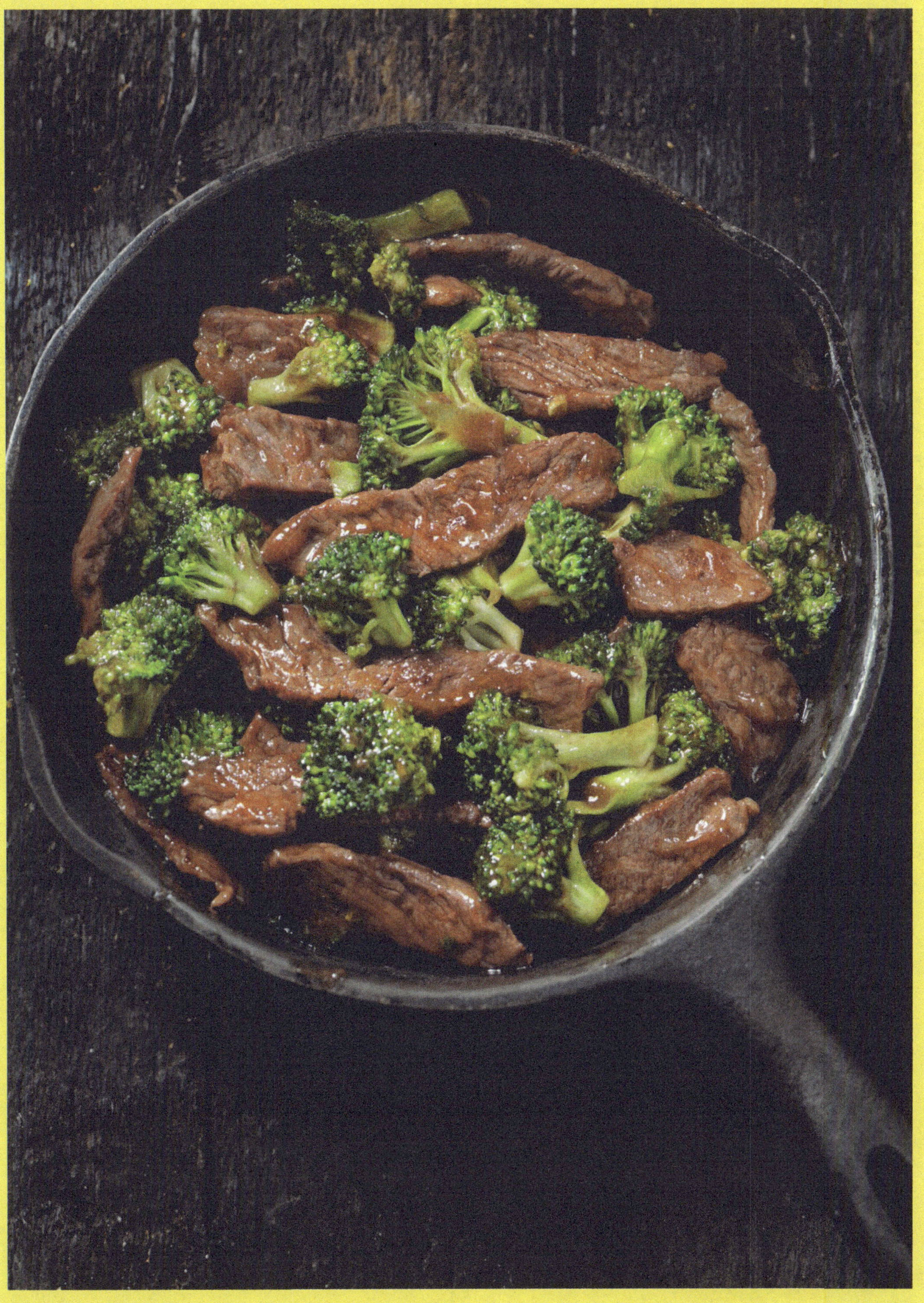

SLOW COOKER CORNED BEEF AND CABBAGE

Prep Time: 10 mins **Cook Time:** 8 hours **Serving:** 6

INGREDIENTS

- 1 (3 to 4 lbs) corned beef brisket, including spice packet
- 4 cups water
- 2 bay leaves
- 1 onion, quartered
- 3 carrots, peeled and cut into pieces
- 6 red potatoes, quartered
- 1 small cabbage head, cut into wedges
- Mustard, for serving

INSTRUCTIONS

1. Put the beef brisket in the slow cooker. Sprinkle the spices from the packet over the brisket. Add bay leaves and ladle water over the meat.
2. Place the onion quarters around the brisket. Cover and cook on low for 8 hours.
3. In the last 2 hours of cooking, add carrot pieces and potatoes to the slow cooker.
4. Add cabbage wedges to the slow cooker in the last hour of cooking.
5. Remove the beef brisket and let it rest for a few minutes before slicing it against the grain.
6. Serve the corned beef with vegetables on the side, accompanied by mustard.

Nutritional Values (per serving):

Calories: 560, Protein: 35g, Carbohydrate: 45g, Fat: 28g

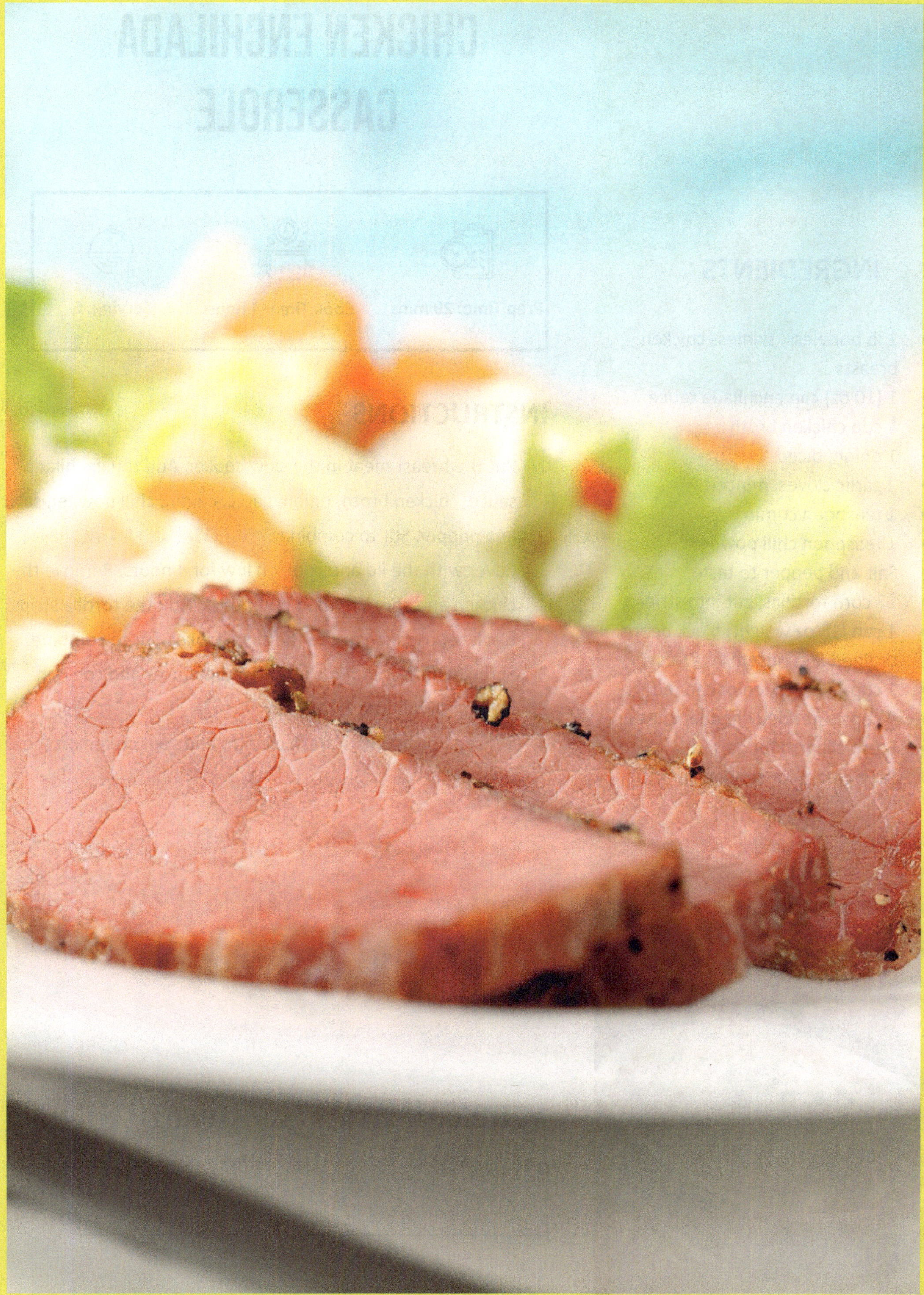

CHICKEN ENCHILADA CASSEROLE

Prep Time: 20 mins **Cook Time:** 4 hours **Serving:** 6

INGREDIENTS

- 1 lb boneless, skinless chicken breasts
- 1 (10 oz) can enchilada sauce
- 1 cup chicken broth
- 1 onion, diced
- 2 garlic cloves, minced
- 1 teaspoon cumin
- 1 teaspoon chili powder
- Salt and pepper to taste
- 12 corn tortillas, cut into strips
- 1 can (15 oz weight) black beans, drained and rinsed
- 1 cup corn (frozen or canned)
- 2 cups shredded cheddar cheese
- Fresh cilantro for garnish
- Sour cream for serving

INSTRUCTIONS

1. Put the breast meat in the slow cooker. Add the enchilada sauce, chicken broth, onion, garlic, cumin, chili powder, salt, and pepper. Stir to combine.
2. Cover with the lid and cook on low for 4 hours. Remove the chicken and shred it, then put it back. Add the tortilla strips, black beans, and corn to the slow cooker. Stir to combine.
3. Sprinkle the shredded cheese on top. Cover and cook on high for 30 minutes.
4. Serve garnished with fresh cilantro and sour cream on the side.

Nutritional Values (per serving):

Calories: 420, Protein: 30g, Carbohydrate: 40g, Fat: 18g

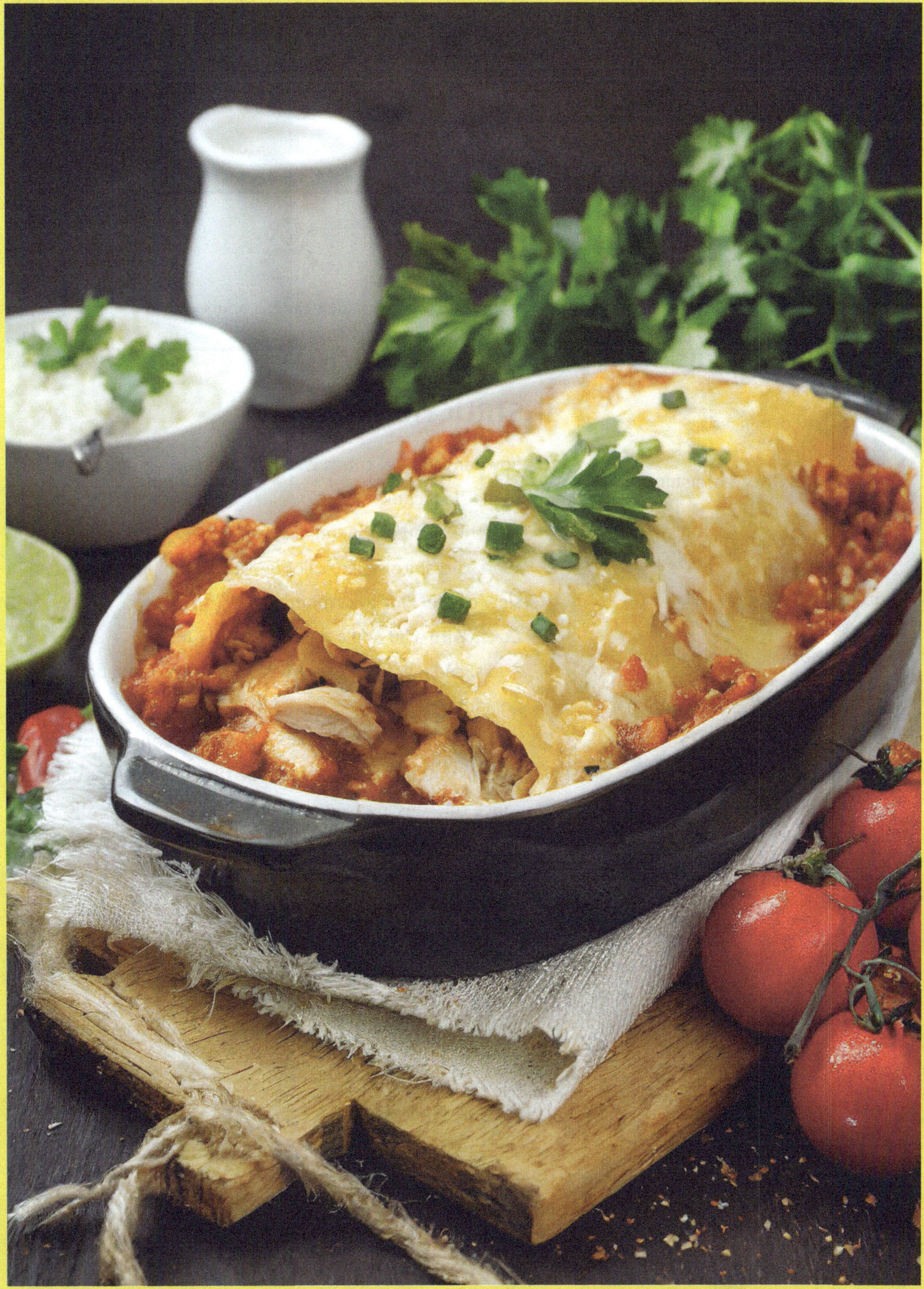

BEEF STROGANOFF

INGREDIENTS

- 2 lb. beef meat, cut into cubes
- Salt and pepper to taste
- 1 onion, diced
- 2 cloves garlic, minced
- 1 cup beef broth
- 2 tablespoons Worcestershire sauce
- 1 tablespoon Dijon mustard
- 1 teaspoon paprika
- 8 ounces mushrooms, sliced
- 1 cup sour cream
- 3 tablespoons all-purpose flour
- Cooked egg noodles for serving
- Fresh parsley, chopped, for garnish

Prep Time: 15 mins **Cook Time: 8 hours** **Serving: 6**

INSTRUCTIONS

1. Powder the beef cubes with salt and pepper and place them in the slow cooker.
2. Add the diced onion, minced garlic, beef broth, Worcestershire sauce, Dijon mustard, and paprika to the slow cooker. Stir to combine.
3. Cover with a lid and cook on low for 7 hours.
4. Add sliced mushrooms to the slow cooker. Cook on low for an additional hour.
5. Toss the sour cream with flour in a bowl until smooth. Stir the mixture and cook on high for 18-20 minutes or until the sauce thickens.
6. Serve the beef stroganoff over cooked egg noodles and garnish with chopped parsley.

Nutritional Values (per serving):

Calories: 460, Protein: 40g, Carbohydrate: 10g, Fat: 28g

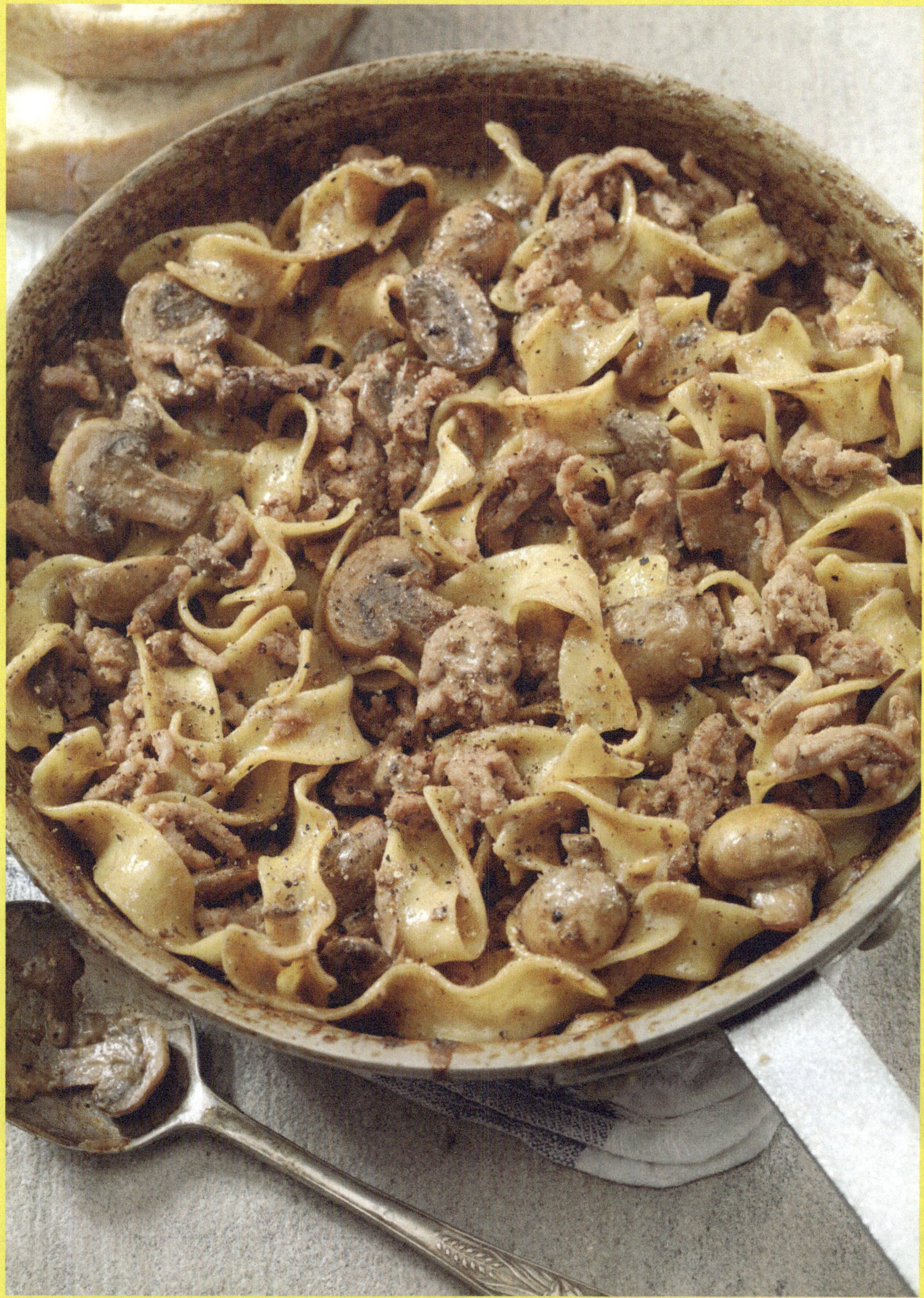

SLOW COOKER CHICKEN CURRY

Prep Time: 20 mins   **Cook Time:** 6 hours   **Serving:** 6

INGREDIENTS

- 2 lb. chicken thighs, without skin & bone, cut into bite-sized pieces
- 1 onion, finely chopped
- 3 cloves garlic, minced
- 1 tablespoon fresh ginger, grated
- 1 can (14 oz) coconut milk
- 2 tablespoons curry powder
- 1 teaspoon ground turmeric
- 1 teaspoon cumin
- 1/2 teaspoon chili powder (adjust to taste)
- 1 can (14 oz) diced tomatoes, undrained
- Salt to taste
- Fresh cilantro, chopped, for garnish
- Cooked rice for serving

INSTRUCTIONS

1. Place the thigh pieces in the slow cooker. Add chopped onion, mashed garlic, grated ginger, coconut milk, curry powder, turmeric, cumin, chili powder, and diced tomatoes. Stir the chicken properly, and ensure it is well coated with spices and liquid. Cover and cook on low for 6 hours until the flavors blend well.
2. Powder it with salt to taste. Serve the chicken curry over cooked rice and garnish with chopped cilantro.

Nutritional Values (per serving):

Calories: 380, Protein: 28g, Carbohydrate: 12g, Fat: 24g

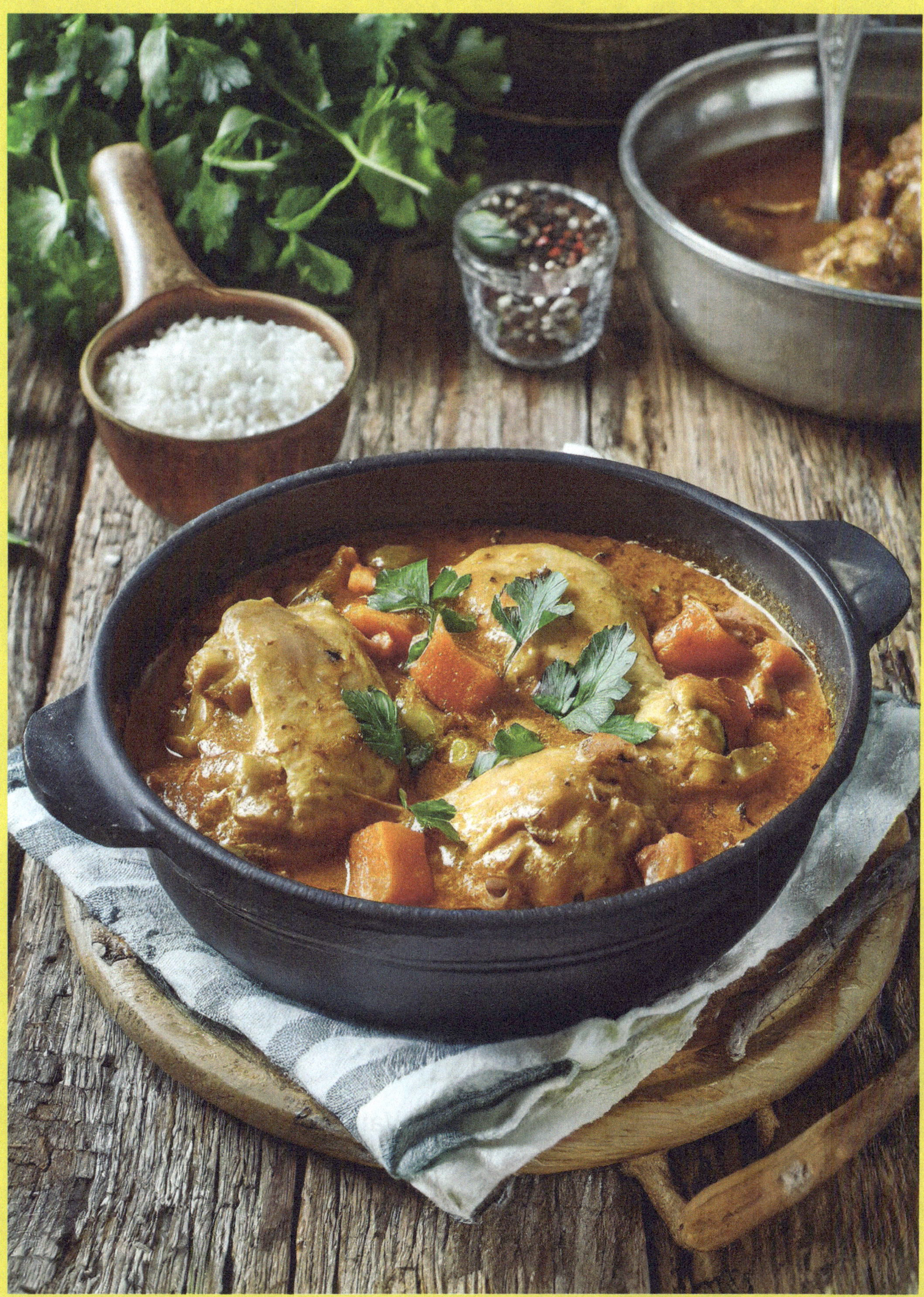

MACARONI AND CHEESE

INGREDIENTS

- 8 ounces elbow macaroni, cooked and drained
- 1 tablespoon unsalted butter
- 1 can (12 oz) evaporated milk
- 1 cup whole milk
- 2 eggs, beaten
- 1/2 teaspoon salt
- 1/4 teaspoon ground black pepper
- 3 cups shredded sharp cheddar cheese
- 1 cup shredded Monterey Jack cheese

Prep Time: 10 mins **Cook Time:** 2-3 hours **Serving:** 6

INSTRUCTIONS

1. Grease the slow cooker's inside (base and walls) with butter.
2. Combine evaporated milk, whole milk, beaten eggs, salt, and pepper in a bowl. Stir in the cooked macaroni, sharp cheddar, and Monterey Jack cheese. Mix well.
3. Pour the macaroni mixture into the slow cooker.
4. Cover and cook on low for 2-3 hours or until the center is set and the edges are slightly browned.
5. Stir the macaroni and cheese before serving to mix the melted cheese evenly.

Nutritional Values (per serving):

Calories: 530, Protein: 28g, Carbohydrate: 35g, Fat: 32g

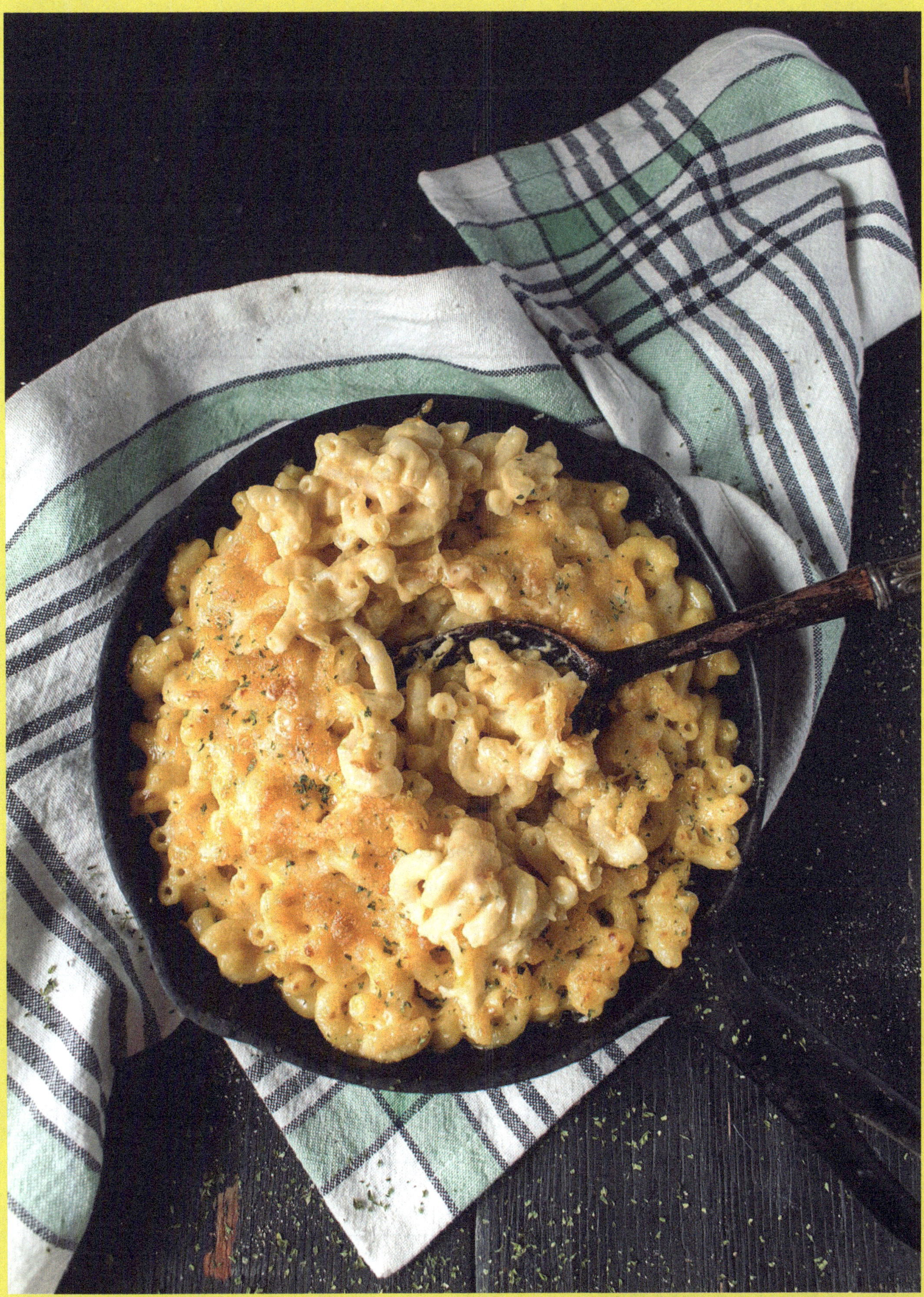

SLOW COOKER PORK CARNITAS

Prep Time: 20 mins   **Cook Time:** 8 hours   **Serving:** 6-8

INGREDIENTS

- 3 lbs pork shoulder (pork butt), trimmed and cut into 2-inch chunks
- 1 tablespoon salt
- 1 teaspoon black pepper
- 2 teaspoons cumin
- 1 teaspoon oregano
- 1/2 teaspoon chili powder
- 4 garlic cloves, minced
- 1 onion, chopped
- 1 orange, juice and zest
- 1 lime, juice only
- 1/2 cup chicken broth

INSTRUCTIONS

1. Mix salt, black pepper, cumin, oregano, and chili powder in a small bowl.
2. Sprinkle the spice mixture and rub over the pork chunks.
3. Throw the seasoned pork in the slow cooker. Add the minced garlic, chopped onion, orange juice and zest, lime juice, and chicken broth.
4. Cover and cook on low for 8 hours. Mix two forks to shred the pork in the slow cooker with the cooking juices.
5. If desired, spread the shredded pork on a baking sheet and broil for a few minutes until the edges become crispy.
6. Serve the carnitas in tacos, burritos, or over rice, garnished with your choice of toppings (e.g., cilantro, diced onion, avocado, lime wedges).

Nutritional Values (per serving):

Calories: 350, Protein: 44g, Carbohydrate: 5g, Fat: 15g

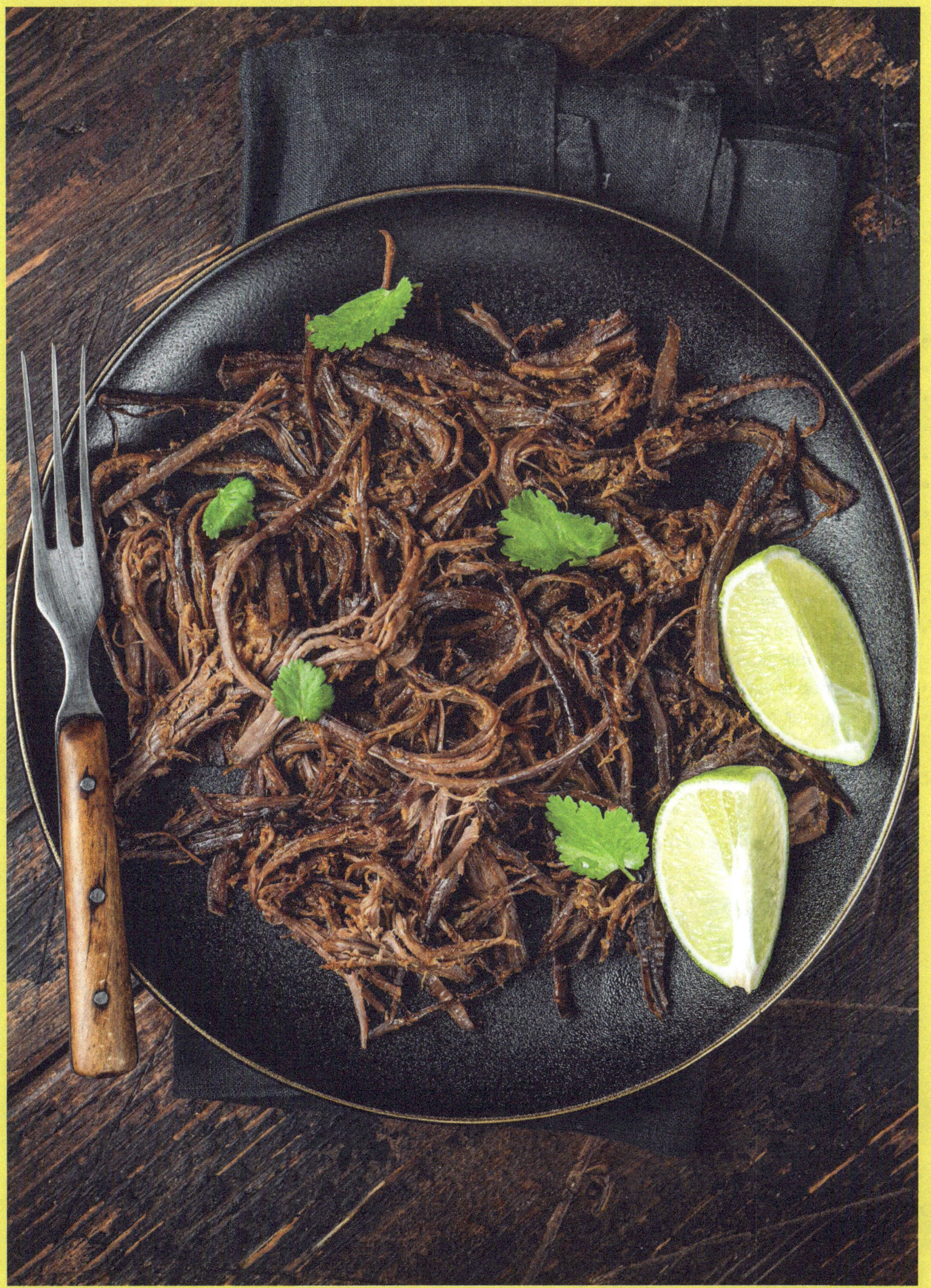

SWEET AND SOUR MEATBALLS

Prep Time: 15 mins   **Cook Time:** 4 hours   **Serving:** 4-6

INGREDIENTS

- 1 lb ground beef
- 1/2 cup breadcrumbs
- 1 egg, beaten
- 1 teaspoon salt
- 1/2 teaspoon black pepper
- 1/2 teaspoon garlic powder
- 1/2 cup onion, finely chopped
- 1 can (20 oz) pineapple chunks in juice, drained (reserve juice)
- 1/2 cup ketchup
- 1/3 cup brown sugar
- 1/3 cup apple cider vinegar
- 2 tablespoons soy sauce
- 1 bell pepper, cut into 1-inch pieces
- 1 tablespoon cornstarch

INSTRUCTIONS

1. Combine ground beef, breadcrumbs, egg, salt, pepper, garlic powder, and onion in a bowl.
2. Mix well and form into 1-inch meatballs. Place the meatballs in the slow cooker.
3. Mix the reserved pineapple juice, ketchup, brown sugar, apple cider vinegar, and soy sauce in another bowl. Pour the mixture over the meatballs.
4. Add the pineapple chunks and bell pepper pieces to the slow cooker. Cover and cook on low for 4 hours.
5. If desired, thicken the sauce by mixing cornstarch with water to form a slurry, then toss it into the slow cooker. Cook on high for 15-20 minutes or until the sauce is thickened.
6. Serve the meatballs with sauce over rice or with your choice of side.

Nutritional Values (per serving):

Calories: 450, Protein: 26g, Carbohydrate: 50g, Fat: 18g

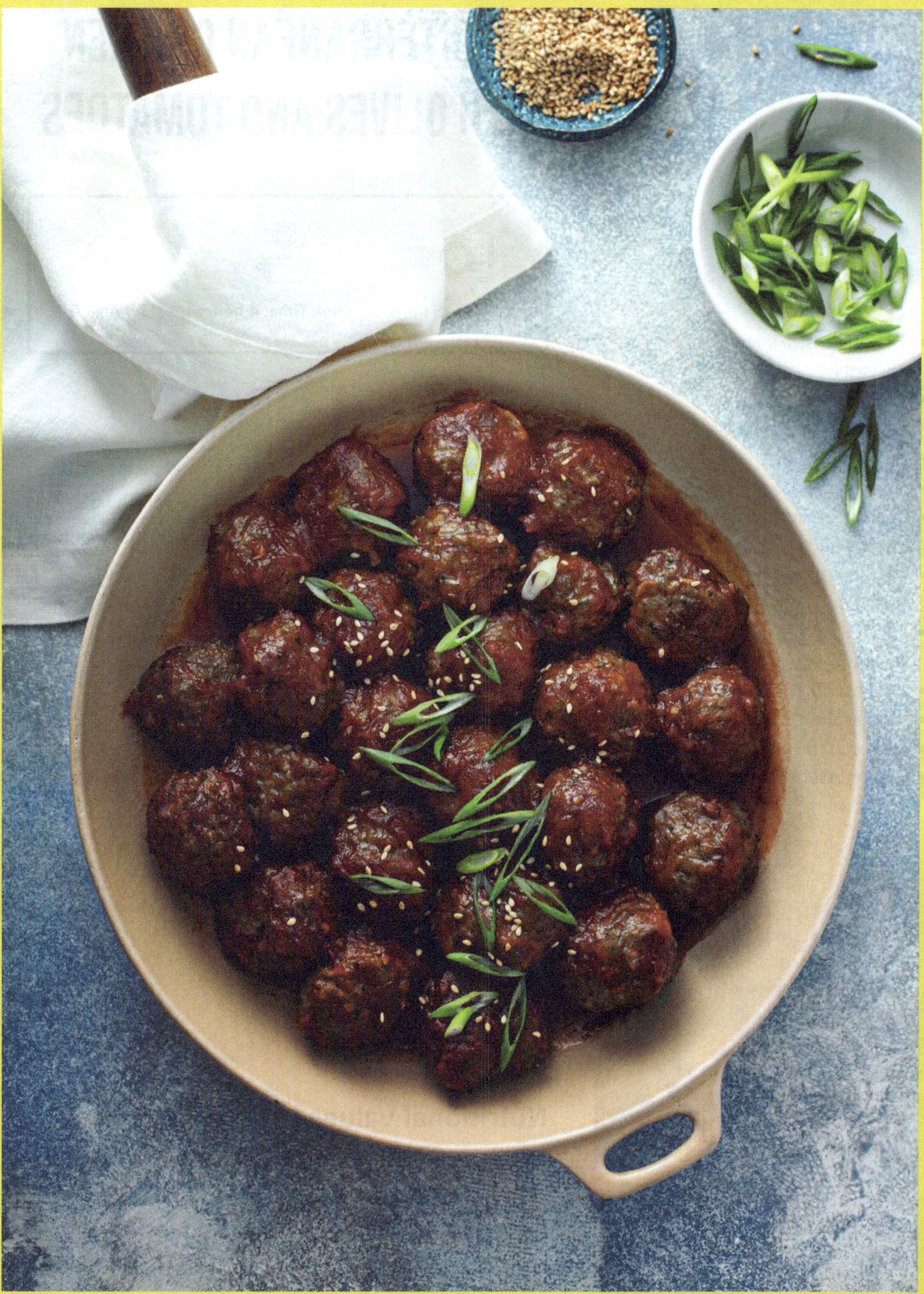

MEDITERRANEAN CHICKEN WITH OLIVES AND TOMATOES

Prep Time: 15 mins   **Cook Time: 4 hours**   **Serving: 4**

INGREDIENTS

- 4 boneless, skinless chicken breasts
- Salt and pepper to taste
- 1 tablespoon olive oil
- 1 onion, thinly sliced
- 3 cloves garlic, minced
- 1 can (14.5 oz) diced tomatoes, undrained
- 1/2 cup pitted Kalamata olives, halved
- 1/2 cup green olives, pitted and halved
- 1 teaspoon dried oregano
- 1 teaspoon dried basil
- 1/4 cup fresh parsley, chopped
- 1/4 cup feta cheese, crumbled (optional)

INSTRUCTIONS

1. Powder the chicken breasts with salt and pepper.
2. Heat one tbsp oil in a skillet over medium-high heat. Add breast meat and brown on both sides, about 3-4 minutes per side. Transfer to the slow cooker.
3. Add onion, ngarlicgarlic, and sauté until softened in the same skillet for about 5 minutes. Transfer to the slow cooker.
4. Add diced tomatoes (with juice), Kalamata olives, green olives, oregano, and basil to the slow cooker. Stir to combine.
5. Cover and cook on low for 4 hours, until chicken is tender and cooked through.
6. If desired, serve the chicken garnished with fresh parsley and crumbled feta cheese.

Nutritional Values (per serving):

Calories: 290, Protein: 31g, Carbohydrate: 9g, Fat: 14g

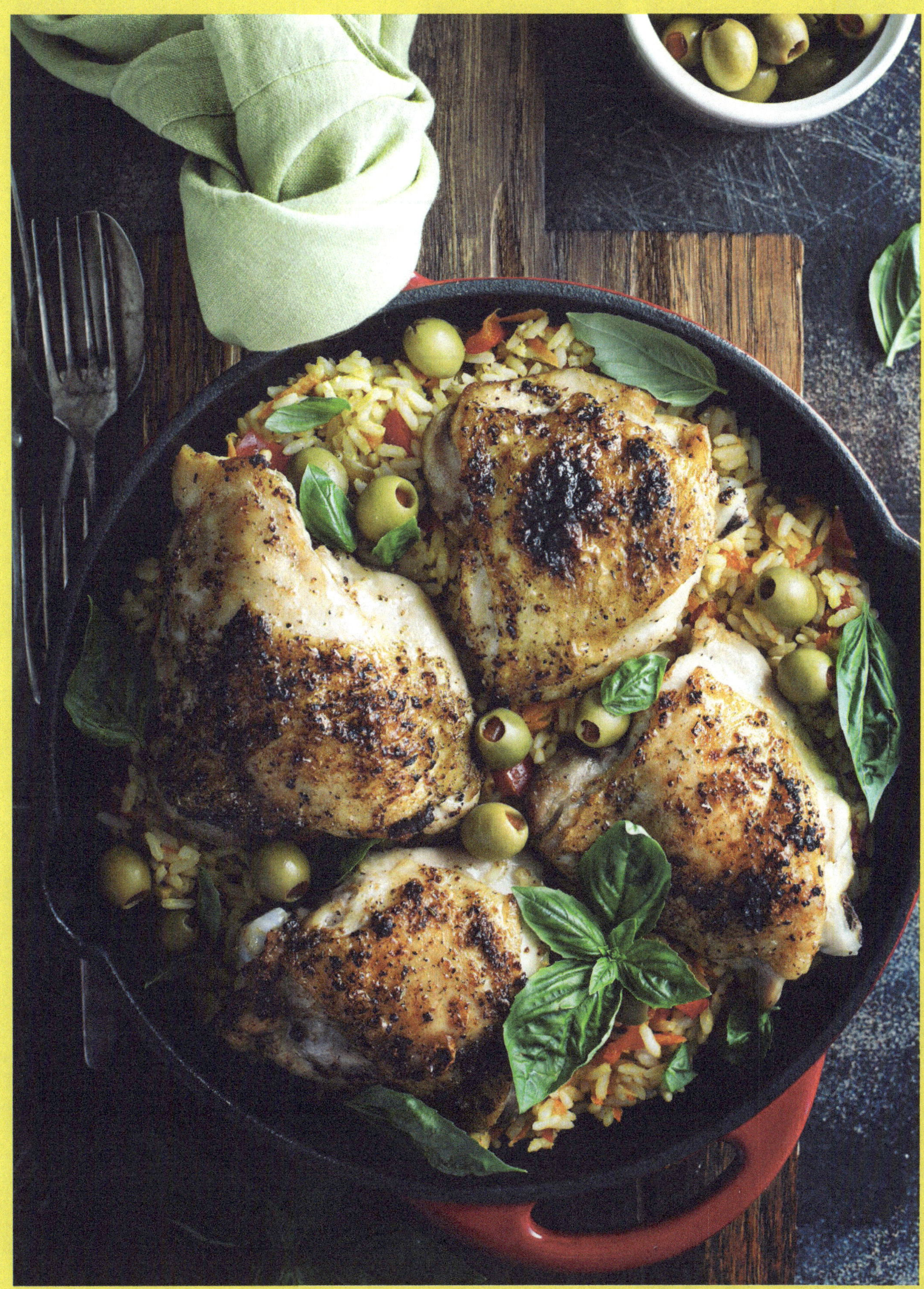

CROCKPOT BEEF STROGANOFF

Prep Time: 20 mins   **Cook Time:** 8 hours   **Serving:** 6

INGREDIENTS

- Two lb. beef stew meat, cut into pieces
- Salt and pepper to taste
- 1 onion, chopped
- 2 cloves garlic, minced
- 1 cup beef broth
- 2 tablespoons Worcestershire sauce
- 1 teaspoon Dijon mustard
- 1 cup sliced mushrooms
- 1 cup sour cream
- 3 tablespoons flour
- 4 tablespoons water
- Cooked egg noodles for serving
- Fresh parsley, chopped, for garnish

INSTRUCTIONS

1. Powder the beef pieces with salt and pepper and place them in the crockpot.
2. Add the chopped onion, minced garlic, beef broth, Worcestershire sauce, and Dijon mustard. Stir to combine.
3. Cover with a lid and cook on low for 7 hours.
4. Add the sliced mushrooms to the crockpot. Cook more on high for 1 hour.
5. Mix the sour cream, flour, and water in a small bowl until smooth. Stir the mixture into the crockpot to thicken the sauce. Cook on high for an additional 30 minutes.
6. Serve the beef stroganoff over cooked egg noodles garnished with fresh parsley.

Nutritional Values (per serving):

Calories: 480, Protein: 40g, Carbohydrate: 15g, Fat: 30g

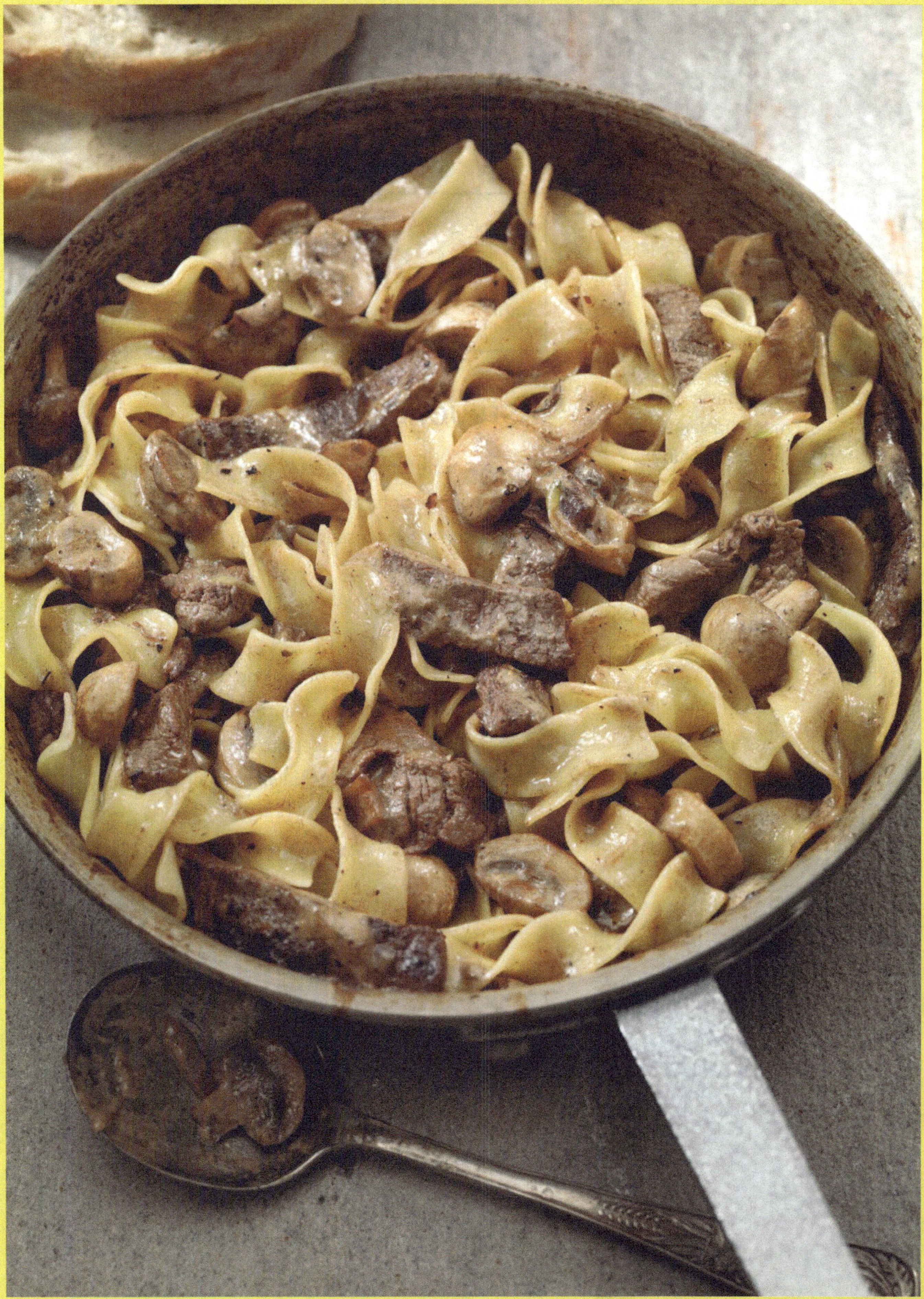

SLOW COOKER CHICKEN PARMESAN

Prep Time: 15 mins | **Cook Time:** 4 hours | **Serving:** 4

INGREDIENTS

- 4 boneless, skinless chicken breasts
- Salt and pepper to taste
- 1 jar (24 oz) marinara sauce
- 1 teaspoon Italian seasoning
- 1 cup shredded mozzarella cheese
- 1/4 cup grated Parmesan cheese
- 1/2 cup Italian breadcrumbs
- Fresh basil, chopped, for garnish

INSTRUCTIONS

1. Powder the chicken breasts with salt and pepper and place them in the bottom of the crockpot.
2. Pour the marinara sauce over the chicken. Sprinkle Italian seasoning on top.
3. Cover and cook on low for 4 hours until chicken is cooked through.
4. In the last 30 minutes of cooking, sprinkle the mozzarella and Parmesan cheeses over the chicken. Cover again and keep heat allow the cheese to melt.
5. Before serving, sprinkle Italian breadcrumbs and fresh basil over the top.
6. Serve the chicken Parmesan with pasta or a side of your choice.

Nutritional Values (per serving):

Calories: 380, Protein: 38g, Carbohydrate: 20g, Fat: 16g

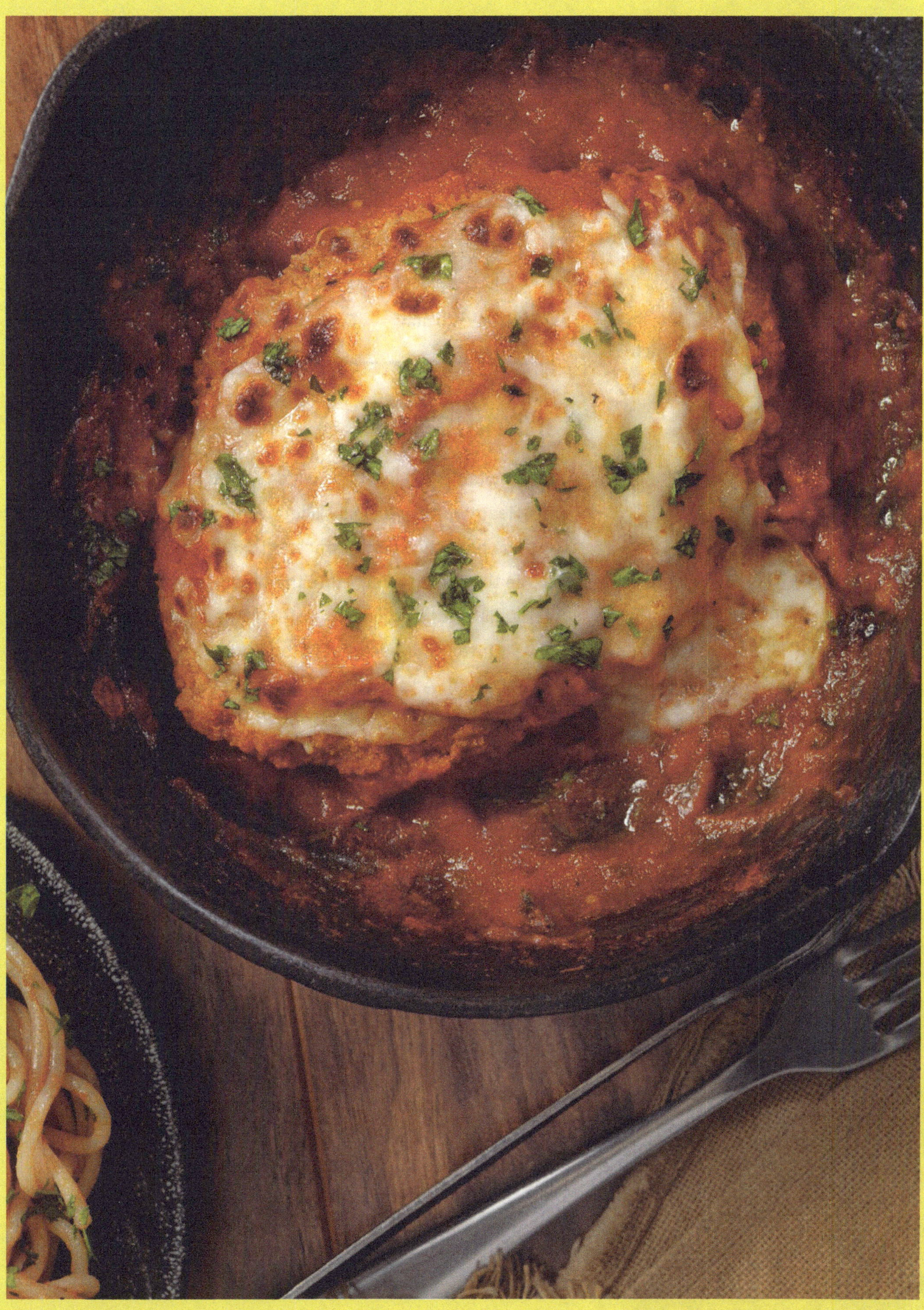

BEEF AND GUINNESS STEW

Prep Time: 20 mins   **Cook Time:** 8 hours   **Serving:** 6

INGREDIENTS

- 2 lbs beef chuck, cut into 1-inch cubes
- Salt and pepper to taste
- 2 tablespoons olive oil
- 1 onion, chopped
- 2 carrots, peeled and sliced
- 2 celery stalks, sliced
- 3 cloves garlic, minced
- 1 can (14.9 oz) Guinness stout
- 2 cups beef broth
- 2 tablespoons tomato paste
- 1 teaspoon sugar
- 1 teaspoon dried thyme
- 2 bay leaves
- 2 tablespoons all-purpose flour
- 2 tablespoons cold water
- Chopped fresh parsley for garnish

INSTRUCTIONS

1. Powder the beef cubes with salt and pepper.
2. Heat two tbsp oil in a skillet over medium-high heat. Brown the beef cubes, then transfer them to the crockpot.
3. In the same skillet, sauté the onion, carrots, celery, and garlic until softened. Transfer the vegetables to the crockpot.
4. Pour the Guinness, beef broth, and tomato paste into the crockpot. Add sugar, thyme, and bay leaves. Stir to combine.
5. Cover with a lid and cook on low for 8 hours until the beef is tender.
6. Mix flour and cold water in a small bowl to create a slurry. Stir into the stew to thicken. Cook on high for an additional 30 minutes.
7. Remove bay leaves and serve garnished with fresh parsley.

Nutritional Values (per serving):

Calories: 500, Protein: 40g, Carbohydrate: 15g, Fat: 30g

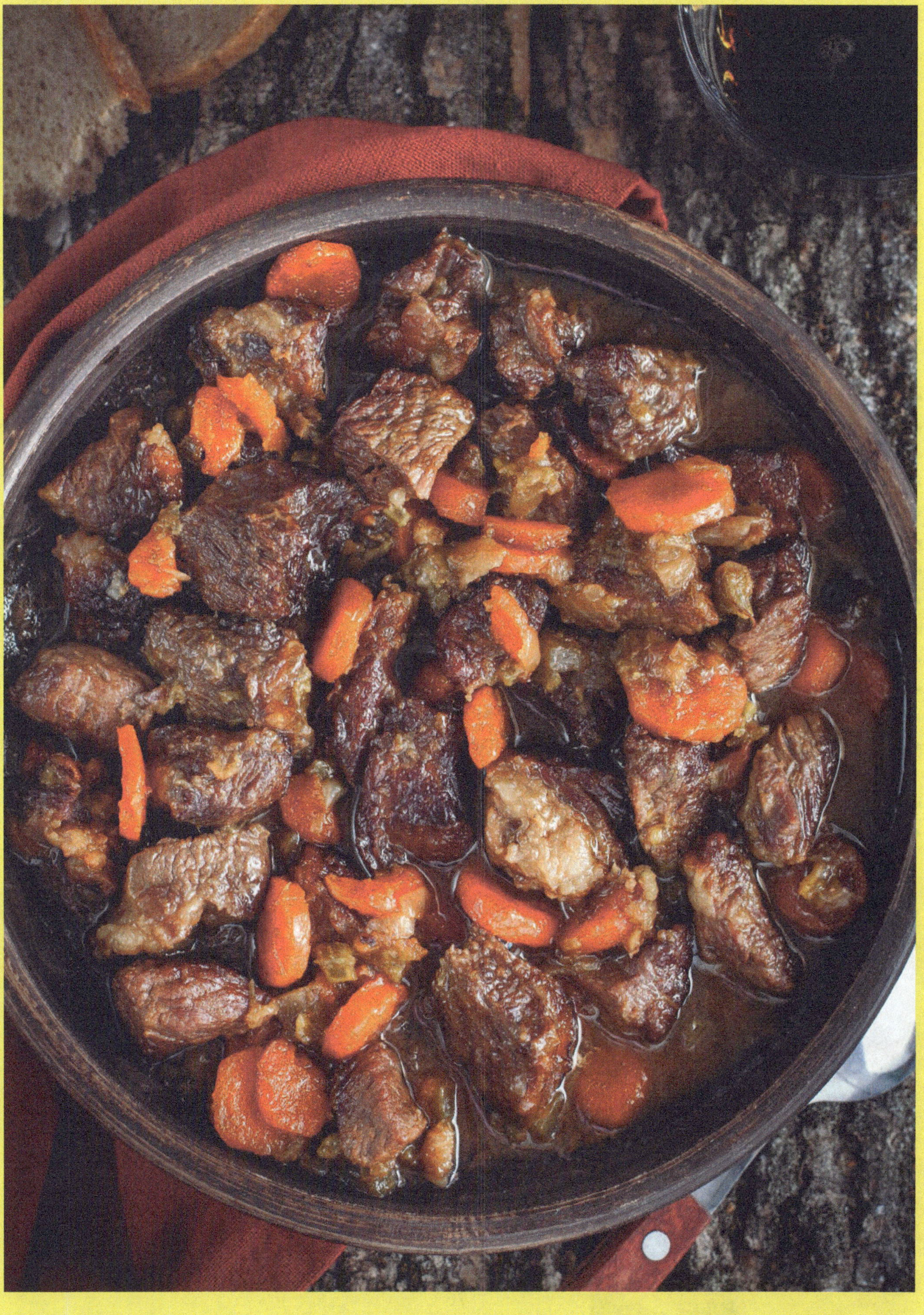

SLOW COOKER THAI PEANUT CHICKEN

Prep Time: 15 mins **Cook Time:** 4 hours **Serving:** 4-6

INGREDIENTS

- 2 lbs boneless, skinless chicken breasts
- Salt and pepper to taste
- 1 red bell pepper, thinly sliced
- 1 onion, thinly sliced
- 4 cloves garlic, minced
- 1/2 cup peanut butter
- 1 cup chicken broth
- 1/4 cup soy sauce
- 2 tablespoons honey
- 2 tablespoons rice vinegar
- 1 tablespoon ginger, grated
- 1 teaspoon crushed red pepper flakes (optional)
- 1/4 cup cilantro, chopped (for garnish)
- Chopped peanuts (for garnish)
- Cooked rice or noodles for serving

INSTRUCTIONS

1. Powder the chicken breasts with salt and crushed pepper and place them in the slow cooker.
2. Add sliced red bell pepper, onion, and garlic over the chicken.
3. Whisk together peanut butter, chicken broth, soy sauce, honey, rice vinegar, grated ginger, and red pepper flakes in a bowl until smooth. Ladle this mixture over the chicken and vegetables in the slow cooker.
4. Cover and cook on low for 4 hours until the chicken is tender and cooked.
5. Shred the chicken, then throw it back into the sauce. Serve over cooked rice or noodles.

Nutritional Values (per serving):

Calories: 475, Protein: 55g, Carbohydrate: 23g, Fat: 20g

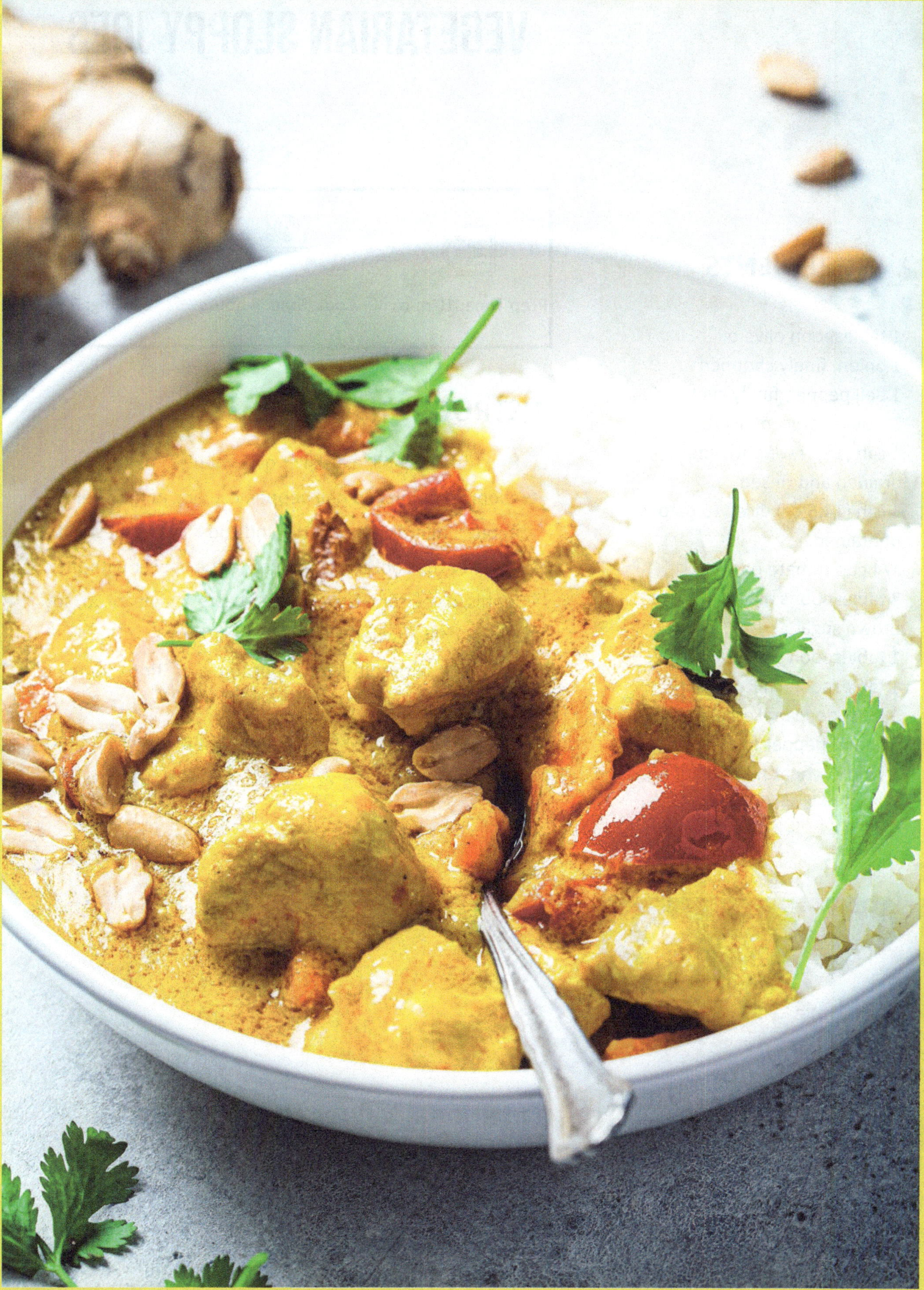

VEGETARIAN SLOPPY JOES

Prep Time: 10 mins   **Cook Time:** 4 hours   **Serving:** 6

INGREDIENTS

- 1 tablespoon olive oil
- 1 onion, finely chopped
- 1 bell pepper, finely chopped
- 3 cloves garlic, minced
- 1 can (15 oz weight) lentils, drained and rinsed
- 1 can (14.5 oz) diced tomatoes, undrained
- 1/4 cup tomato paste
- 2 tablespoons maple syrup or brown sugar
- 1 tablespoon soy sauce
- 1 tablespoon chili powder
- 1 teaspoon smoked paprika
- Salt and pepper to taste
- 6 whole wheat hamburger buns

INSTRUCTIONS

1. Heat one tbsp oil in a skillet over medium heat. Add chopped onion and bell pepper, cooking until softened, about 5 minutes. Add garlic and cook for another minute.
2. Transfer the cooked vegetables to the cooker with the lentils, diced tomatoes, tomato paste, maple syrup, soy sauce, chili powder, and smoked paprika.
3. Powder it with salt and pepper to taste. Stir to combine. Cover and cook on low for 4 hours.
4. Spoon the lentil mixture onto hamburger buns and serve.

Nutritional Values (per serving):

Calories: 320, Protein: 12g, Carbohydrate: 60g, Fat: 5g

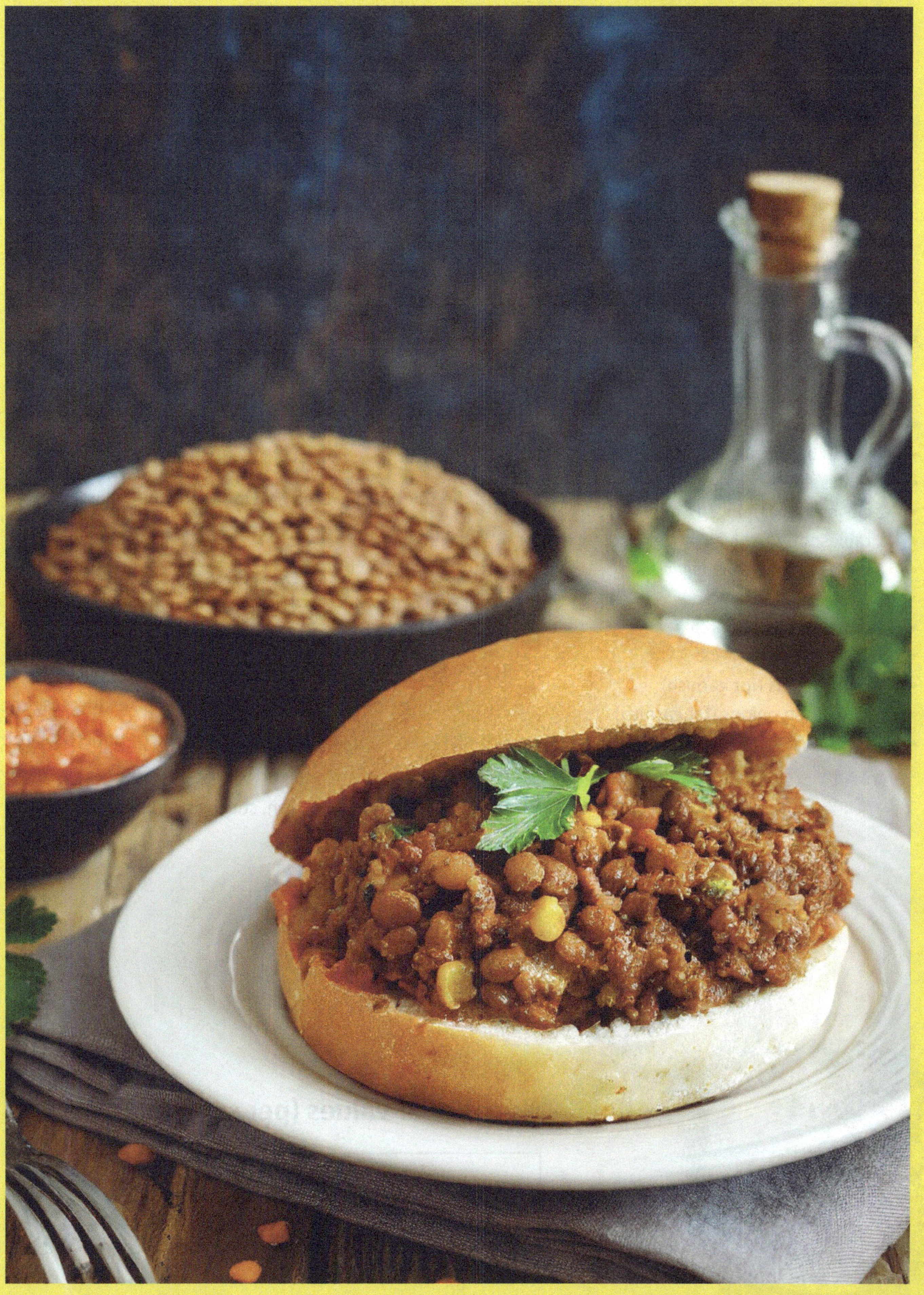

SLOW COOKER CHICKEN TERIYAKI

Prep Time: 15 mins **Cook Time:** 4 hours **Serving:** 4

INGREDIENTS

- 2 lbs boneless, skinless chicken breasts
- 1/2 cup soy sauce
- 1/4 cup water
- 1/4 cup brown sugar
- 2 tablespoons honey
- 2 cloves garlic, minced
- 1 tablespoon fresh ginger, grated
- 2 tablespoons rice vinegar
- 1 tablespoon sesame oil
- 2 teaspoons cornstarch
- 2 teaspoons water
- Sesame seeds (for garnish)
- Sliced green onions (for garnish)
- Cooked rice for serving

INSTRUCTIONS

1. Place chicken breasts in the slow cooker.
2. Toss the soy sauce, water, brown sugar, honey, garlic, grated ginger, vinegar, and sesame oil in a shallow bowl. Pour this mixture over the chicken.
3. Cover and cook on low for 4 hours until chicken is tender.
4. Remove chicken to shred with two forks. Set aside.
5. Toss the cornstarch with water in a small bowl until smooth. Stir this slurry into the sauce in the slow cooker. Increase the setting to high and cook for 15-20 minutes or until the sauce has thickened.
6. Return the shredded chicken, stirring to coat it in the sauce.
7. Serve over cooked rice.

Nutritional Values (per serving):

Calories: 365, Protein: 48g, Carbohydrate: 23g, Fat: 8g

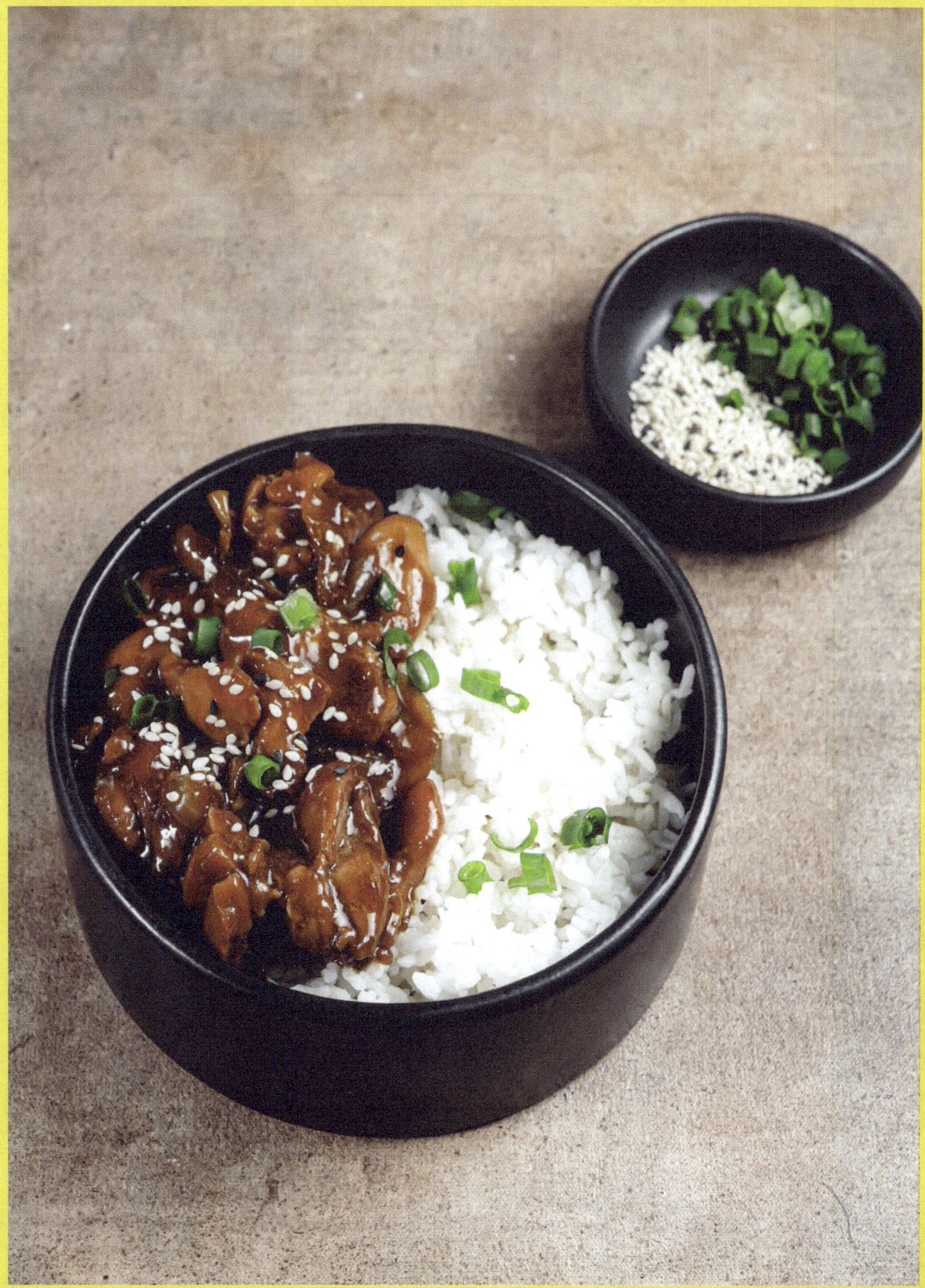

CROCKPOT CHICKEN ALFREDO PASTA

Prep Time: 15 mins **Cook Time:** 4 hours **Serving:** 6

INGREDIENTS

- 1.5 lb. boneless, skinless chicken breasts
- Salt and pepper to taste
- 3 cloves garlic, minced
- 1 cup chicken broth
- 1 cup heavy cream
- 1/2 cup grated Parmesan cheese
- 1/2 teaspoon Italian seasoning
- 1/4 teaspoon ground nutmeg
- 12 oz fettuccine pasta, broken in half
- 2 tablespoons unsalted butter
- Additional grated Parmesan cheese for serving
- Fresh parsley, chopped, for garnish

INSTRUCTIONS

1. Powder chicken breasts with salt and crushed pepper, then place them in the crockpot.
2. Add minced garlic and chicken broth. Cover and cook on low for 4 hours until chicken is cooked through.
3. Remove chicken, shred or cut into bite-sized pieces, and set aside.
4. Stir in heavy cream, grated Parmesan, Italian seasoning, and nutmeg into the juices left in the crockpot. Add the fettuccine and ensure it is submerged in the liquid.
5. Cover and cook on high for 30 minutes.
6. Once the pasta is done, add the shredded chicken and butter back to the crockpot. Stir until the butter is melted and the chicken is heated through.
7. Serve hot, garnished with additional grated Parmesan and fresh parsley.

Nutritional Values (per serving):

Calories: 580, Protein: 38g, Carbohydrate: 44g, Fat: 28g

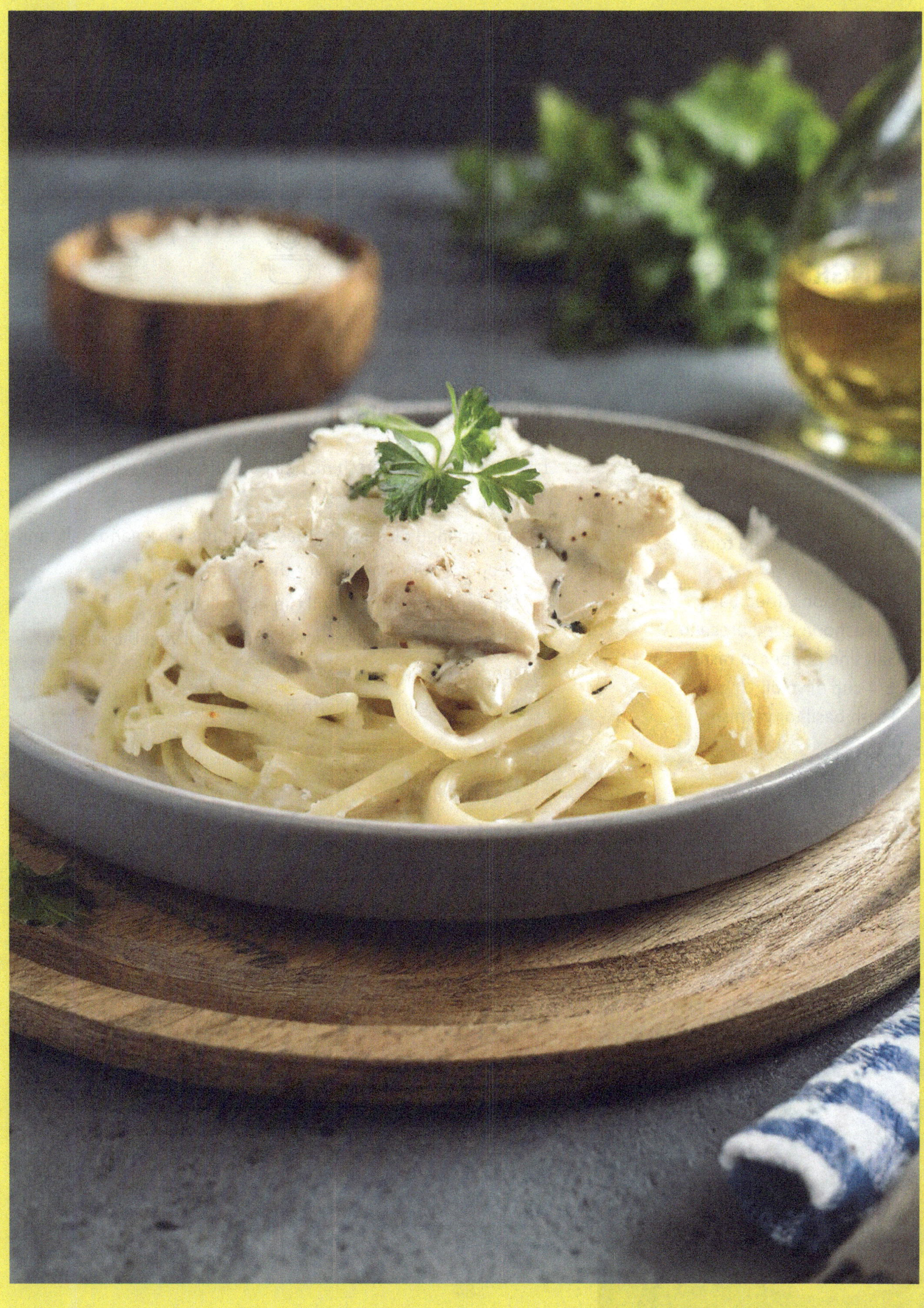

SLOW COOKER RATATOUILLE

Prep Time: 20 mins **Cook Time:** 6 hours **Serving:** 6

INGREDIENTS

- 1 eggplant, cut into 1/2-inch pieces
- 2 zucchinis, sliced
- 2 bell peppers (1 red, 1 yellow), chopped
- 1 onion, chopped
- 3 cloves garlic, minced
- 1 can (28 oz) diced tomatoes, drained
- 2 teaspoons dried basil
- 1 teaspoon dried oregano
- Salt and pepper to taste
- 1/4 cup olive oil
- Fresh basil for garnish

INSTRUCTIONS

1. Place eggplant, zucchini, bell peppers, onion, and garlic in the crockpot.
2. Add drained diced tomatoes, dried basil, oregano, salt, and pepper. Pour olive oil over the vegetables.
3. Stir gently to combine all the ingredients.
4. Cover and cook on low for 6 hours until vegetables are tender.
5. Serve hot, garnished with fresh basil leaves.

Nutritional Values (per serving):

Calories: 180, Protein: 4g, Carbohydrate: 23g, Fat: 10g

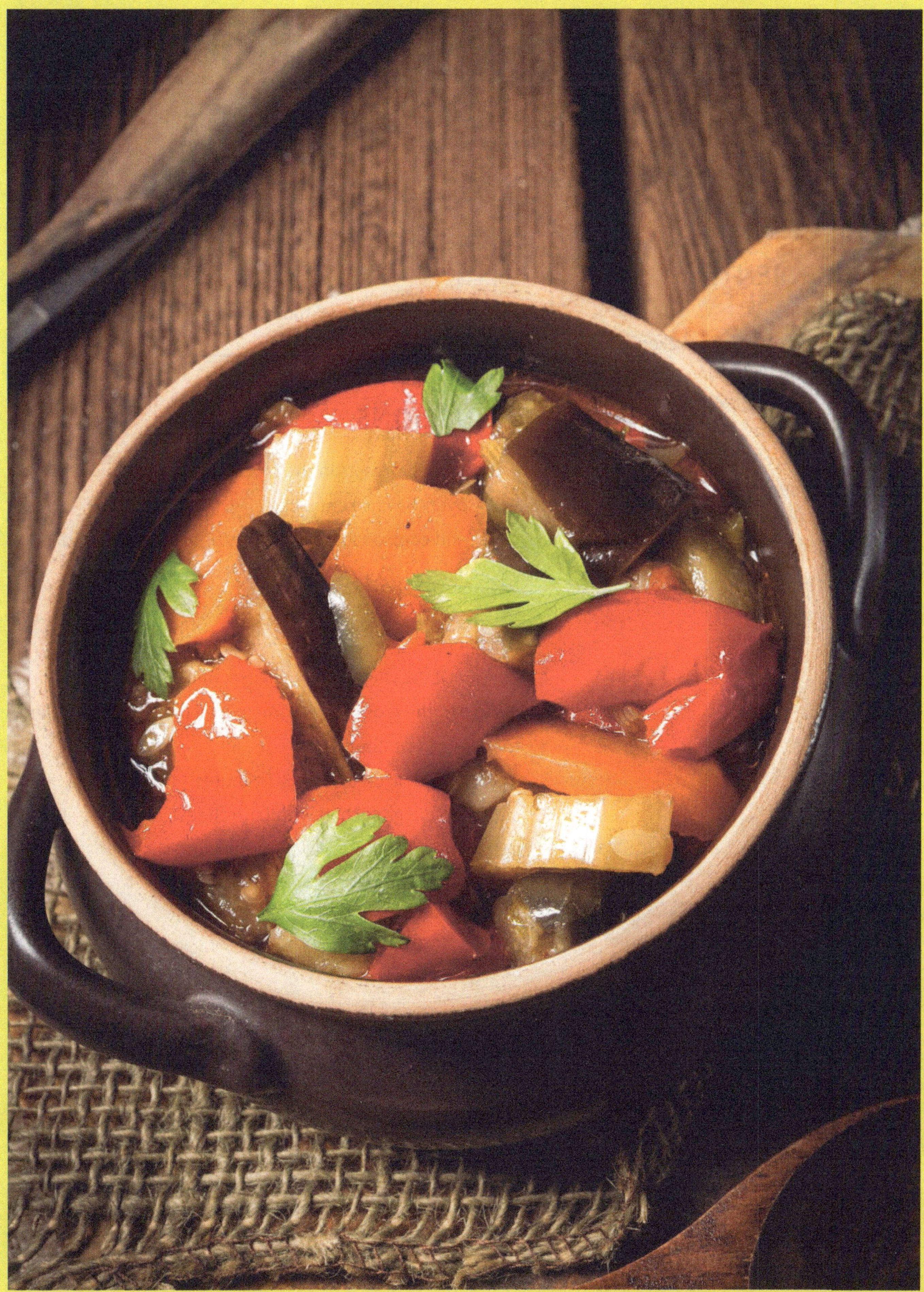

BUFFALO CHICKEN DIP

Prep Time: 10 mins **Cook Time:** 2 hours **Serving:** 8

INGREDIENTS

- 2 lbs boneless, skinless chicken breasts
- 1 cup Buffalo wing sauce
- 1/2 cup ranch dressing
- 1/2 cup cream cheese, softened
- 1 cup shredded cheddar cheese
- Blue cheese crumbles for serving
- Sliced green onions for garnish
- Tortilla chips or celery sticks for serving

INSTRUCTIONS

1. Place chicken breasts in the crockpot. Pour Buffalo wing sauce over the chicken.
2. Cover and cook on low for 2 hours until chicken is cooked through.
3. Remove the chicken to shred it, and return it to the crockpot.
4. Add ranch dressing, cream cheese, and shredded cheddar cheese to the crockpot. Stir them well until combined, and the cheese is melted.
5. Cover and cook on low for 30 minutes.
6. Serve the dip garnished with blue cheese crumbles, sliced green onions, and tortilla chips or celery sticks.

Nutritional Values (per serving):

Calories: 350, Protein: 28g, Carbohydrate: 2g, Fat: 26g

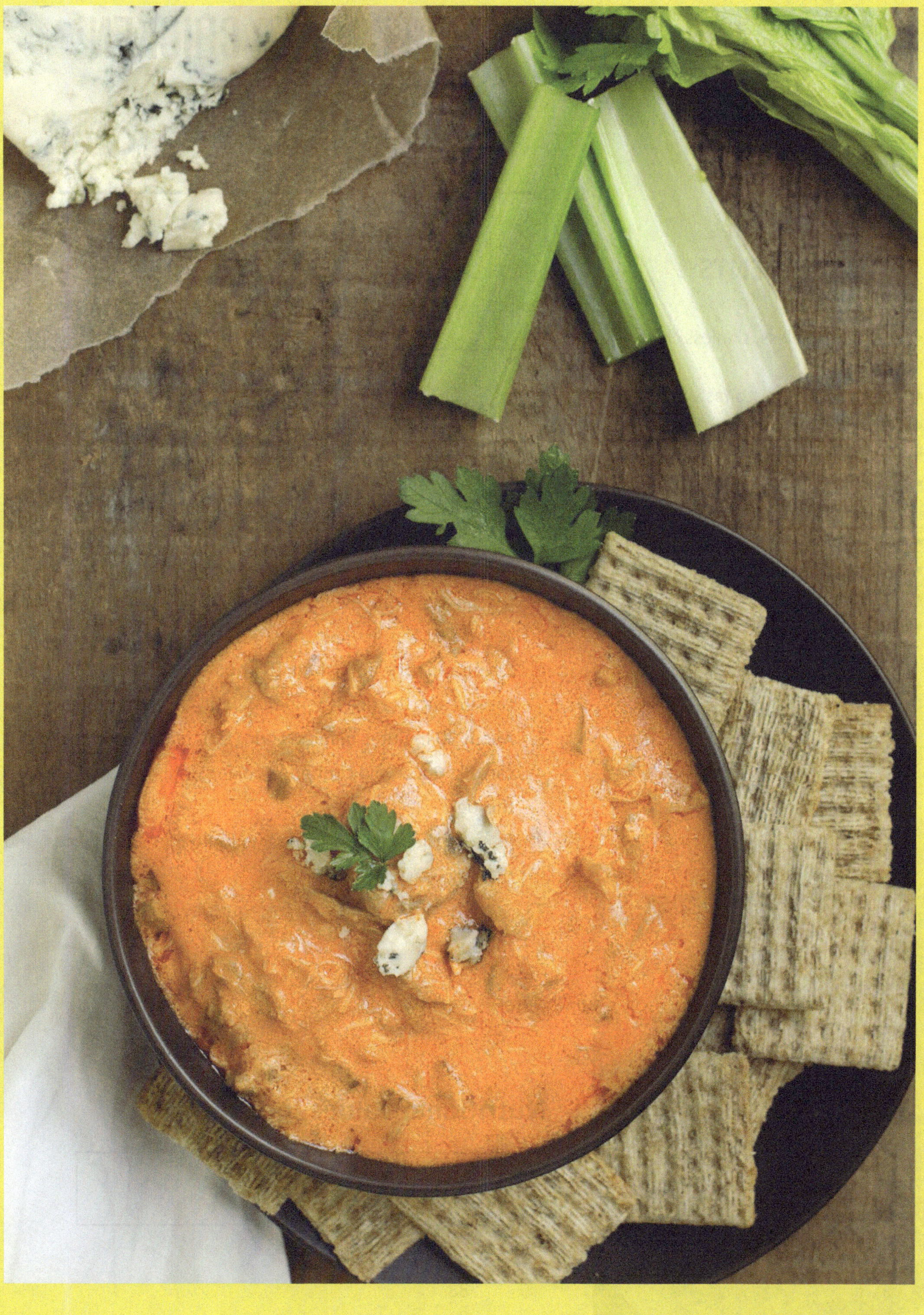

SLOW COOKER CHICKEN AND RICE

Prep Time: 15 mins   **Cook Time:** 4 hours   **Serving:** 6

INGREDIENTS

- 1.5 lb. boneless, skinless chicken breasts
- Salt and pepper to taste
- 1 onion, chopped
- 2 cloves garlic, minced
- 1.5 cups long-grain white rice, rinsed
- 3 cups chicken broth
- 1 teaspoon dried thyme
- 1/2 teaspoon paprika
- 1 cup frozen peas and carrots mix
- Fresh parsley, chopped, for garnish

INSTRUCTIONS

1. Season chicken breasts with salt and pepper, and place them in the bottom of the slow cooker.
2. Add the chopped onion and minced garlic over the chicken.
3. Sprinkle the rinsed rice around and over the chicken. Pour the chicken broth evenly over the rice. Sprinkle thyme and paprika on top.
4. Cover and cook on high for 3-4 hours or until the chicken is cooked and the rice is tender.
5. About 30 minutes before serving, stir in the frozen peas and carrots. Cover and continue cooking until they are heated through.
6. Remove the chicken, shred or cut into bite-sized pieces, and then mix back into the rice.
7. Serve hot, garnished with fresh parsley.

Nutritional Values (per serving):

Calories: 350, Protein: 33g, Carbohydrate: 40g, Fat: 5g

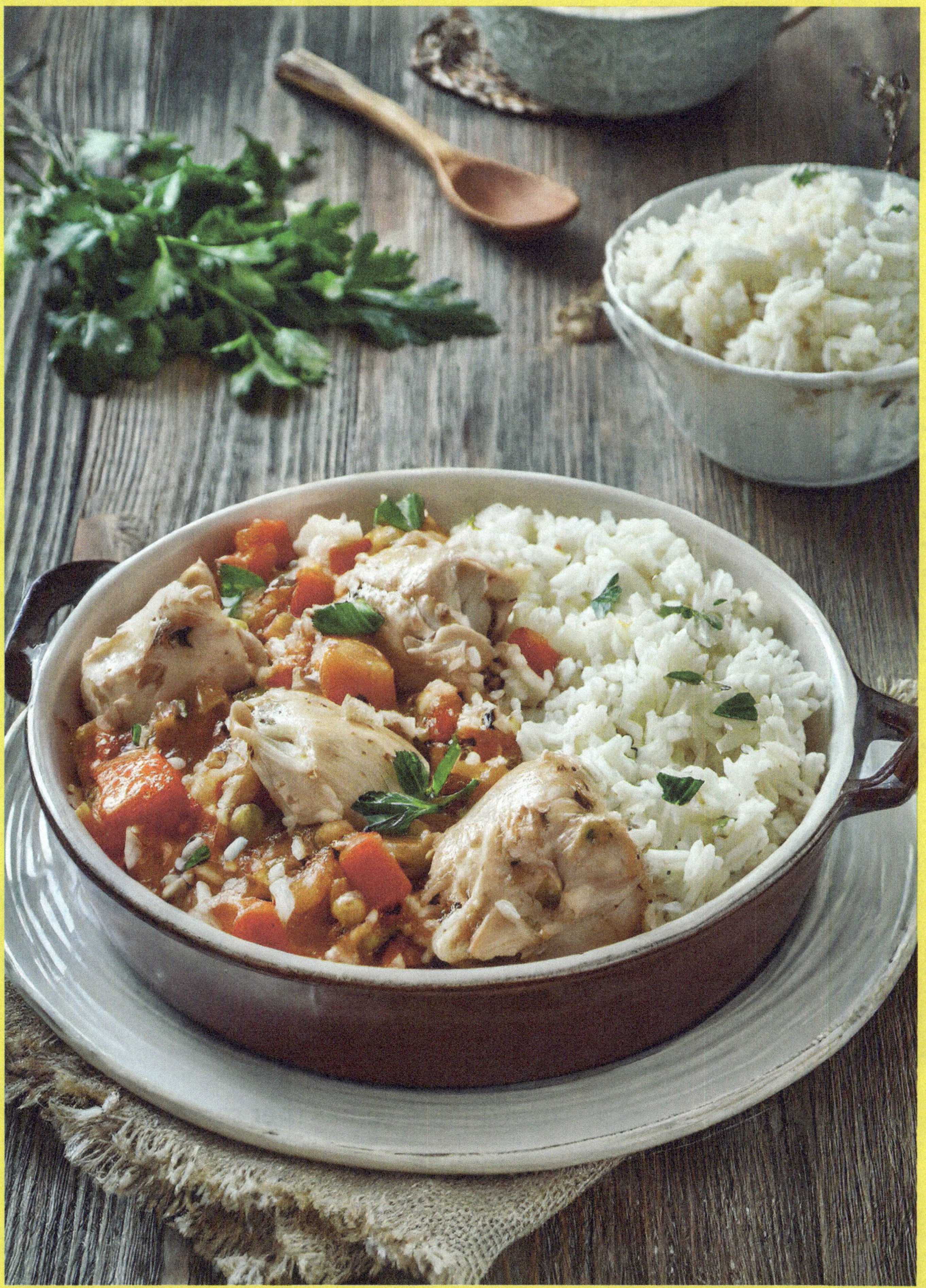

SLOW COOKER VEGETARIAN LASAGNA

Prep Time: 25 mins   **Cook Time:** 4 hours   **Serving:** 8

INGREDIENTS

- 1 jar (24 oz) marinara sauce
- 1 can (15 oz) crushed tomatoes
- 2 cups ricotta cheese
- 1/4 cup grated Parmesan cheese
- 1 tablespoon dried Italian seasoning
- Salt and pepper to taste
- 1 egg, beaten
- 1 box (10 oz) no-boil lasagna noodles
- 1 zucchini, thinly sliced
- 1 bell pepper, thinly sliced
- 2 cups shredded mozzarella cheese
- Fresh basil leaves for garnish

INSTRUCTIONS

1. In a bowl, mix the marinara sauce and crushed tomatoes together. Set aside.
2. Combine ricotta cheese, Parmesan cheese, Italian seasoning, salt, pepper, and egg in another bowl. Mix well.
3. Spread tomato sauce mixture layer (a thin la) on the bottom of the slow cooker.
4. Arrange a layer of no-boil lasagna noodles over the sauce.
5. Spread the ricotta mixture over the noodles, then add a layer of zucchini and bell pepper slices. Sprinkle the shredded mozzarella cheese layer on top.
6. Repeat the layering process until all ingredients are used, finishing with a layer of mozzarella cheese.
7. Cover with the lid and cook on low for 4 hours. Cool the lasagna 12-15 minutes before serving. Garnish with fresh basil leaves.

Nutritional Values (per serving):

Calories: 380, Protein: 22g, Carbohydrate: 35g, Fat: 18g

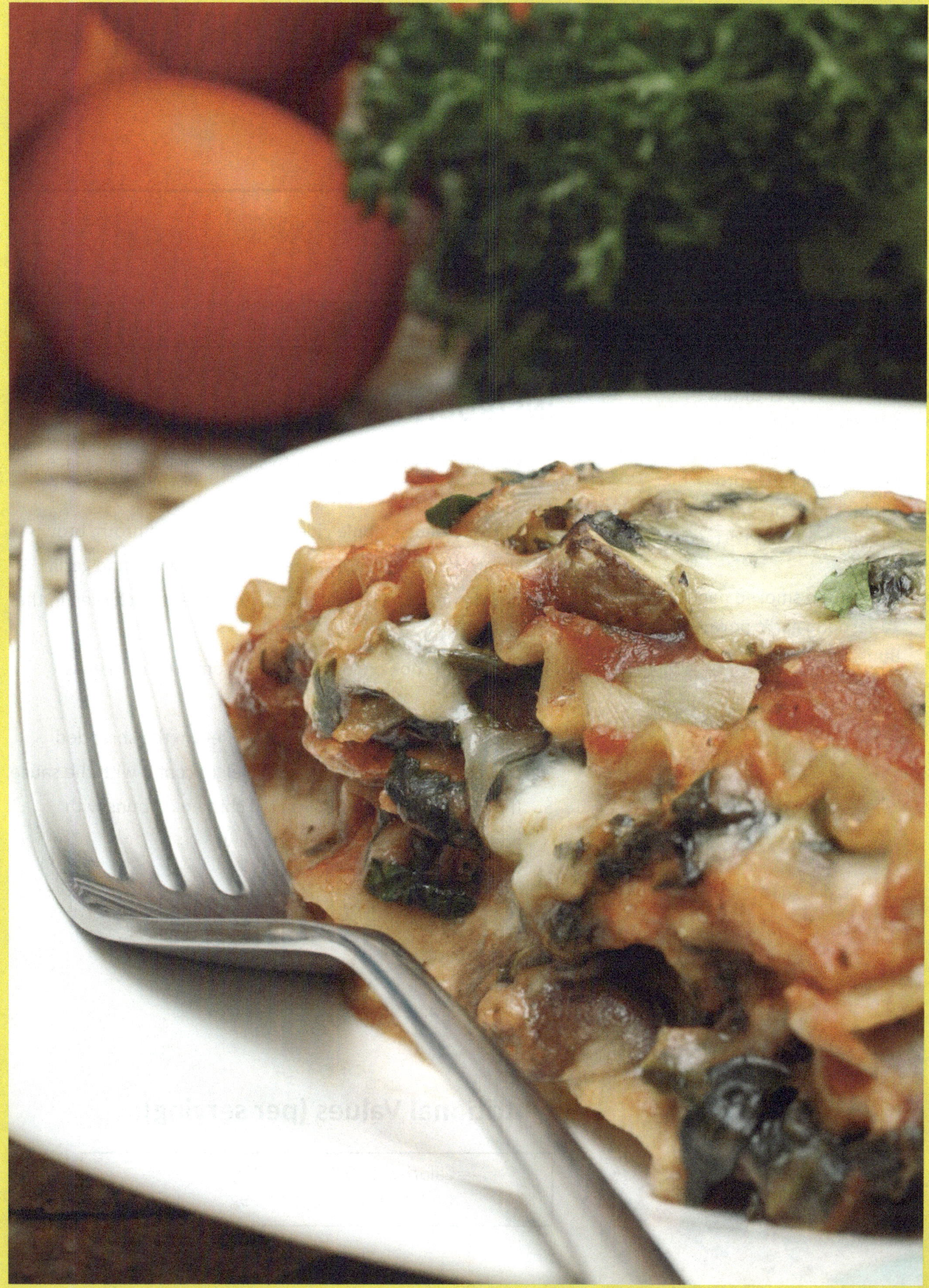

BBQ PULLED CHICKEN

Prep Time: 10 mins **Cook Time:** 4 hours **Serving:** 6

INGREDIENTS

- 2 lbs boneless, skinless chicken breasts
- Salt and pepper to taste
- 1 cup BBQ sauce
- 1/2 cup apple cider vinegar
- 1/2 cup chicken broth
- 1 tablespoon brown sugar
- 1 tablespoon Worcestershire sauce
- 1 teaspoon smoked paprika
- 1 teaspoon garlic powder
- Buns, for serving
- Coleslaw, for serving

INSTRUCTIONS

1. Powder the breast meat with salt and pepper and place them in the slow cooker.
2. Mix BBQ sauce, apple cider vinegar, chicken broth, brown sugar, Worcestershire sauce, smoked paprika, and garlic powder in a bowl. Drop the mixture over the chicken in the slow cooker.
3. Cover and cook on low for 4 hours until the chicken is tender.
4. Remove the chicken and shred it. Return the shredded chicken to the cooker and toss well to coat it with the sauce.
5. If desired, serve the BBQ-pulled chicken on buns with additional BBQ sauce and coleslaw.

Nutritional Values (per serving):

Calories: 330, Protein: 33g, Carbohydrate: 25g, Fat: 9g

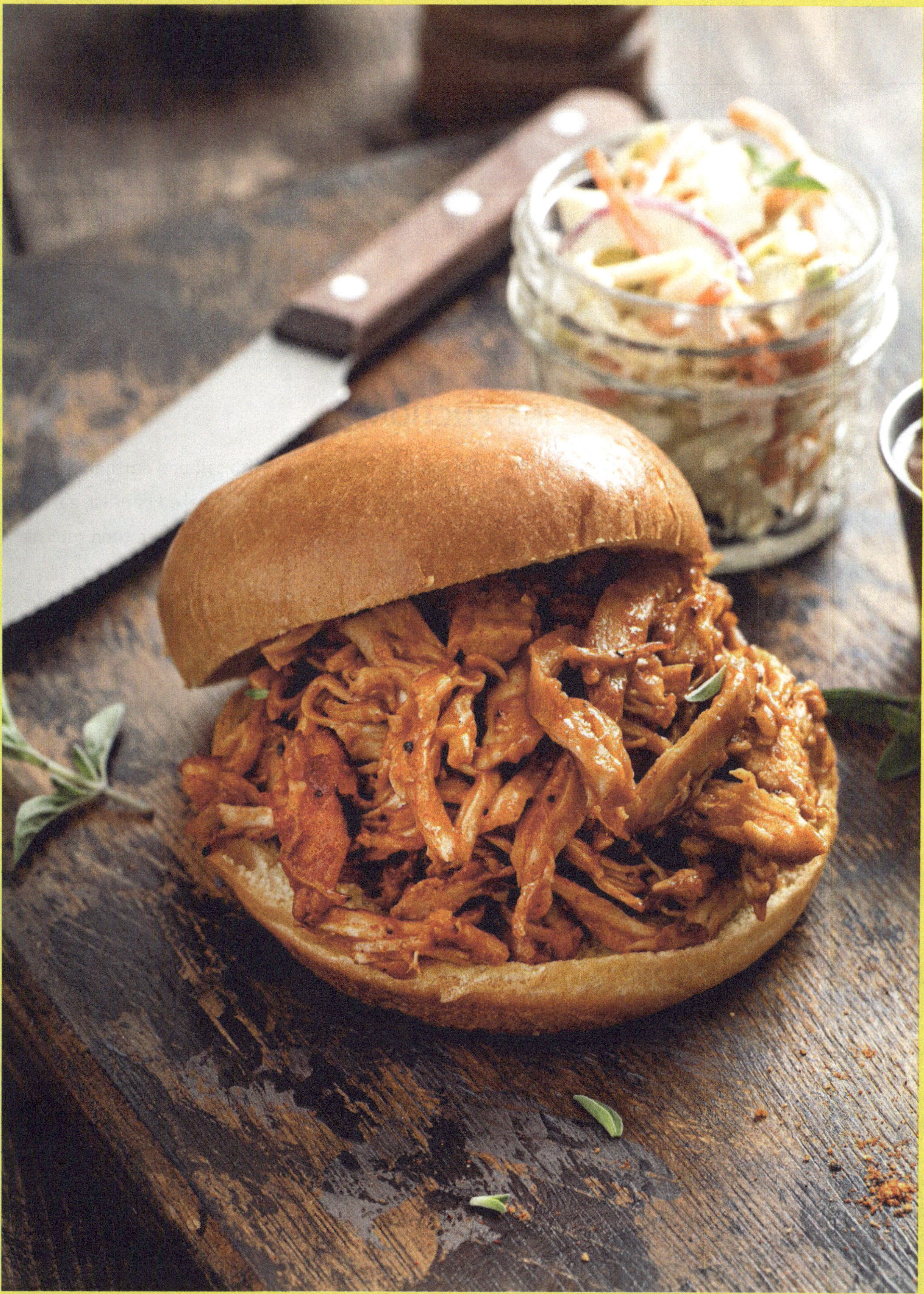

SLOW COOKER BEEF TACOS

INGREDIENTS

- 2 lbs beef chuck roast
- Salt and pepper to taste
- 1 tablespoon chili powder
- 1 teaspoon cumin
- 1 teaspoon smoked paprika
- 1/2 teaspoon garlic powder
- 1/2 teaspoon onion powder
- 1/4 teaspoon cayenne pepper (optional)
- 1 cup beef broth
- 1 lime, juiced
- Corn or flour tortillas for serving
- Toppings: diced tomatoes, shredded lettuce, shredded cheese, sour cream, guacamole

Prep Time: 20 mins **Cook Time:** 8 hours **Serving:** 6

INSTRUCTIONS

1. Powder the beef chuck roast with salt and crushed pepper. Combine the chili powder, cumin, smoked paprika, garlic powder, onion powder, and cayenne pepper, then rub this mixture all over the beef.
2. Transfer the seasoned beef to the slow cooker. Pour beef broth around the beef, then sprinkle the lime juice.
3. Cover with the lid and cook on low for 7-8 hours.
4. Shred the beef and mix with the juices in the slow cooker.
5. Serve the shredded beef in tortillas with your choice of toppings.

Nutritional Values (per serving):

Calories: 330, Protein: 35g, Carbohydrate: 2g, Fat: 20g

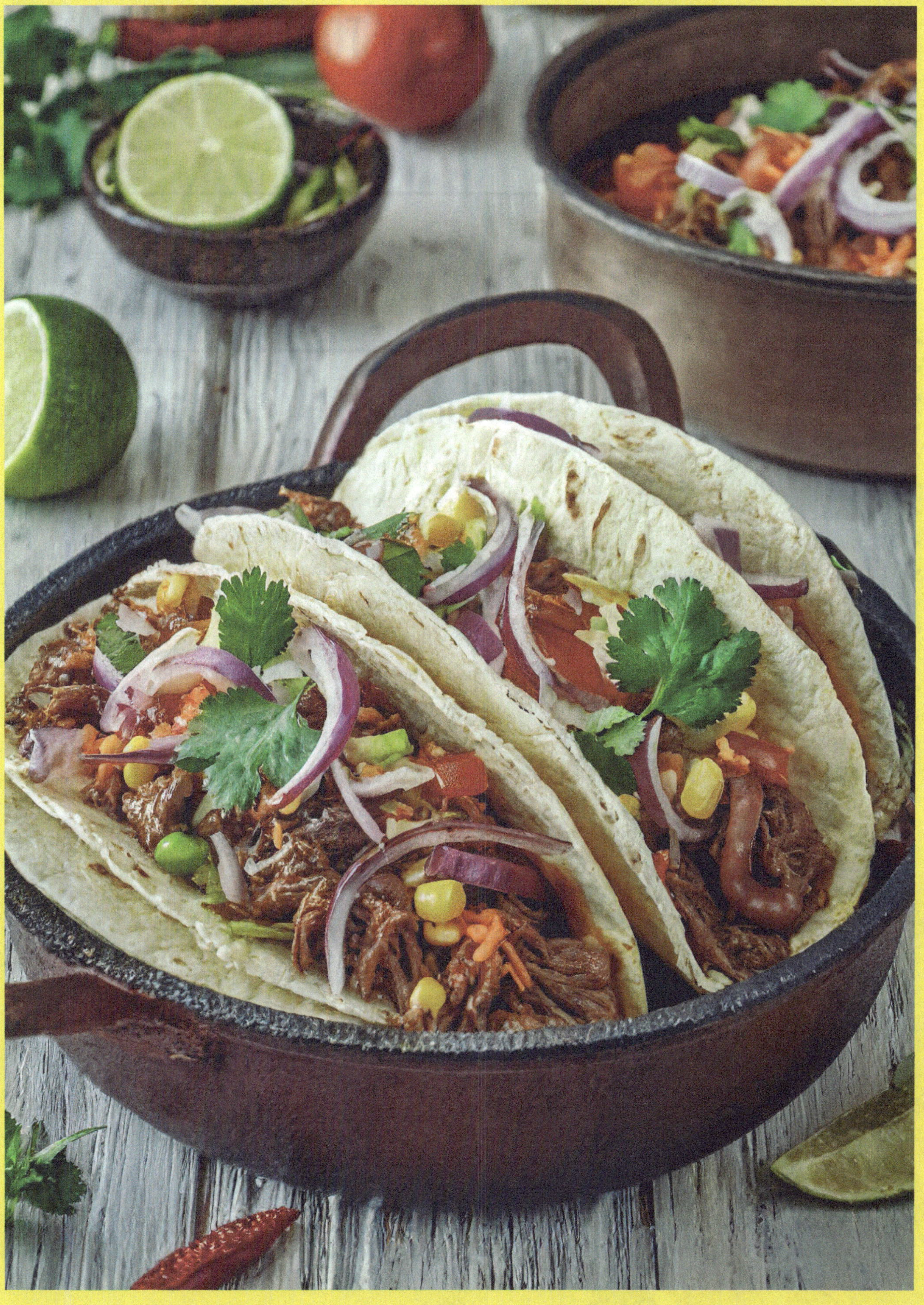

CREAMY TORTELLINI SOUP

Prep Time: 15 mins   **Cook Time:** 4 hours   **Serving:** 6

INGREDIENTS

- 1 tablespoon olive oil
- 1 onion, diced
- 2 carrots, peeled and diced
- 2 stalks celery, diced
- 3 cloves garlic, minced
- 1 teaspoon Italian seasoning
- Salt and pepper to taste
- 4 cups vegetable broth
- 1 can (14.5 oz) diced tomatoes, undrained
- 1 package (9 oz) refrigerated cheese tortellini
- 1 cup heavy cream
- 2 cups fresh spinach, chopped
- Grated Parmesan cheese for serving

INSTRUCTIONS

1. Heat one tbsp oil in a skillet over medium heat. Add onion, carrots, and celery, cooking until softened, about 5 minutes. Add mashed garlic, Italian seasoning, salt, and crushed pepper, and cook for another minute. Transfer the mixture to the slow cooker.
2. Add vegetable broth and diced tomatoes to the slow cooker. Stir to combine. Cover and cook on low for 4 hours.
3. Increase the heat to high. Stir in the tortellini and cook for 15-20 minutes or until tender.
4. Stir in the heavy cream and spinach, cooking until the spinach is wilted.
5. Serve hot, sprinkled with grated Parmesan cheese.

Nutritional Values (per serving):

Calories: 390, Protein: 14g, Carbohydrate: 34g, Fat: 22g

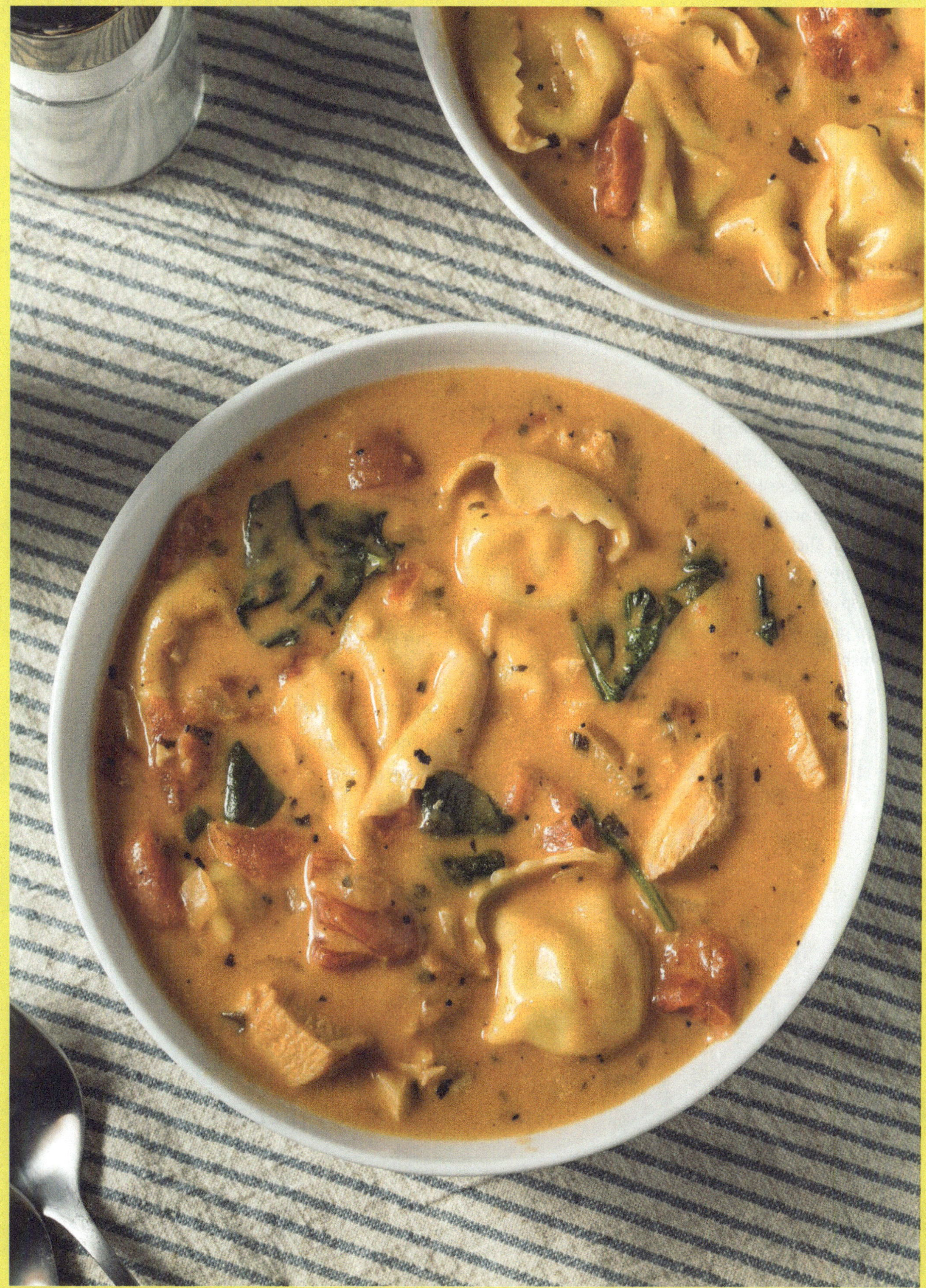

LEMON GARLIC CHICKEN

Prep Time: 10 mins **Cook Time:** 4 hours **Serving:** 4

INGREDIENTS

- 4 boneless, skinless chicken breasts
- Salt and pepper to taste
- 2 tablespoons olive oil
- 3 cloves garlic, minced
- 1/4 cup chicken broth
- 1/4 cup lemon juice
- 1 lemon, sliced
- 1 teaspoon dried oregano
- 1 teaspoon dried thyme
- Fresh parsley, chopped, for garnish

INSTRUCTIONS

1. Season chicken breasts with salt and pepper. Heat two tbsp oil in a skillet over medium-high heat. Add chicken and saute on both sides, about 3-4 minutes per side. Transfer to the slow cooker.
2. Add minced garlic, chicken broth, and lemon juice over the chicken in the slow cooker. Place lemon slices on top of the chicken.
3. Sprinkle oregano and thyme over the chicken.
4. Cover and cook on low for 4 hours until the chicken is cooked through and tender.
5. Serve the chicken garnished with fresh parsley and additional lemon slices if desired.

Nutritional Values (per serving):

Calories: 210, Protein: 26g, Carbohydrate: 3g, Fat: 10g

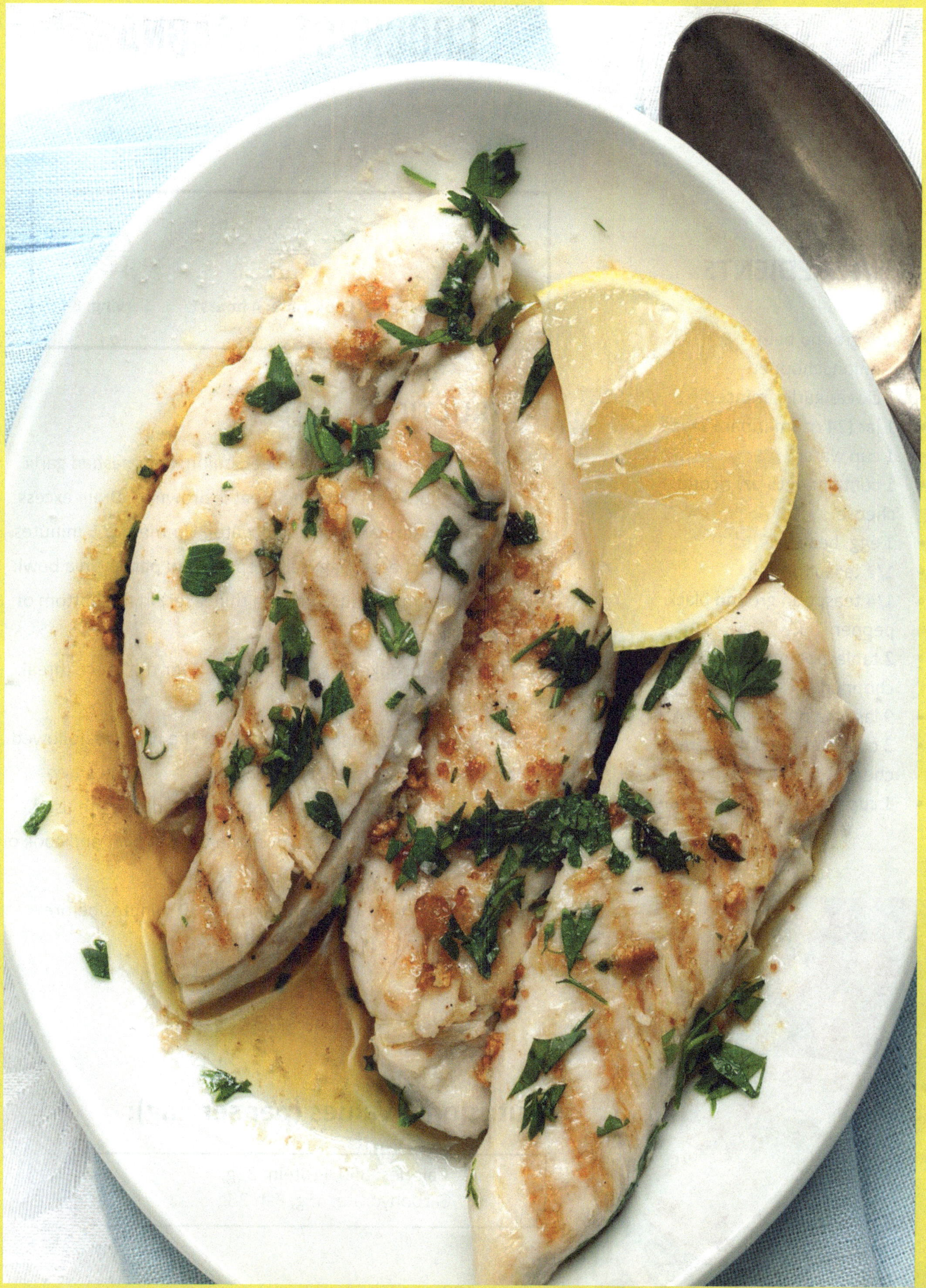

CROCKPOT LASAGNA

Prep Time: 30 mins **Cook Time: 4 hours** **Serving: 8**

INGREDIENTS

- 1 lb ground beef
- 1 onion, chopped
- 2 cloves garlic, minced
- 1 jar (24 oz) marinara sauce
- 1 cup water
- 1 container (15 oz) ricotta cheese
- 1 egg, beaten
- 1/2 teaspoon salt
- 1/4 teaspoon ground black pepper
- 2 tablespoons fresh parsley, chopped
- 9 lasagna noodles, uncooked
- 3 cups shredded mozzarella cheese
- 1 cup grated Parmesan cheese

INSTRUCTIONS

1. In a skillet, prepare ground beef, onion, and mashed garlic over medium heat until the meat is browned. Drain excess fat. Stir in marinara sauce and water. Simmer for 5 minutes.
2. Mix ricotta cheese, egg, salt, pepper, and parsley in a bowl.
3. Spread the meat sauce layer (a thin layer) in the bottom of the crockpot.
4. Place the uncooked lasagna noodles over the sauce (break noodles to fit).
5. Spread the ricotta mixture layer over the noodles, followed by a layer of mozzarella cheese.
6. Repeat the layering process until all ingredients are used.
7. Sprinkle Parmesan cheese over the top. ssCover and cook on low for 4 hours until noodles are tender.
8. Let lasagna stand in the crockpot for 10 minutes before serving.

Nutritional Values (per serving):

Calories: 550, Protein: 35g, Carbohydrate: 45g, Fat: 28g

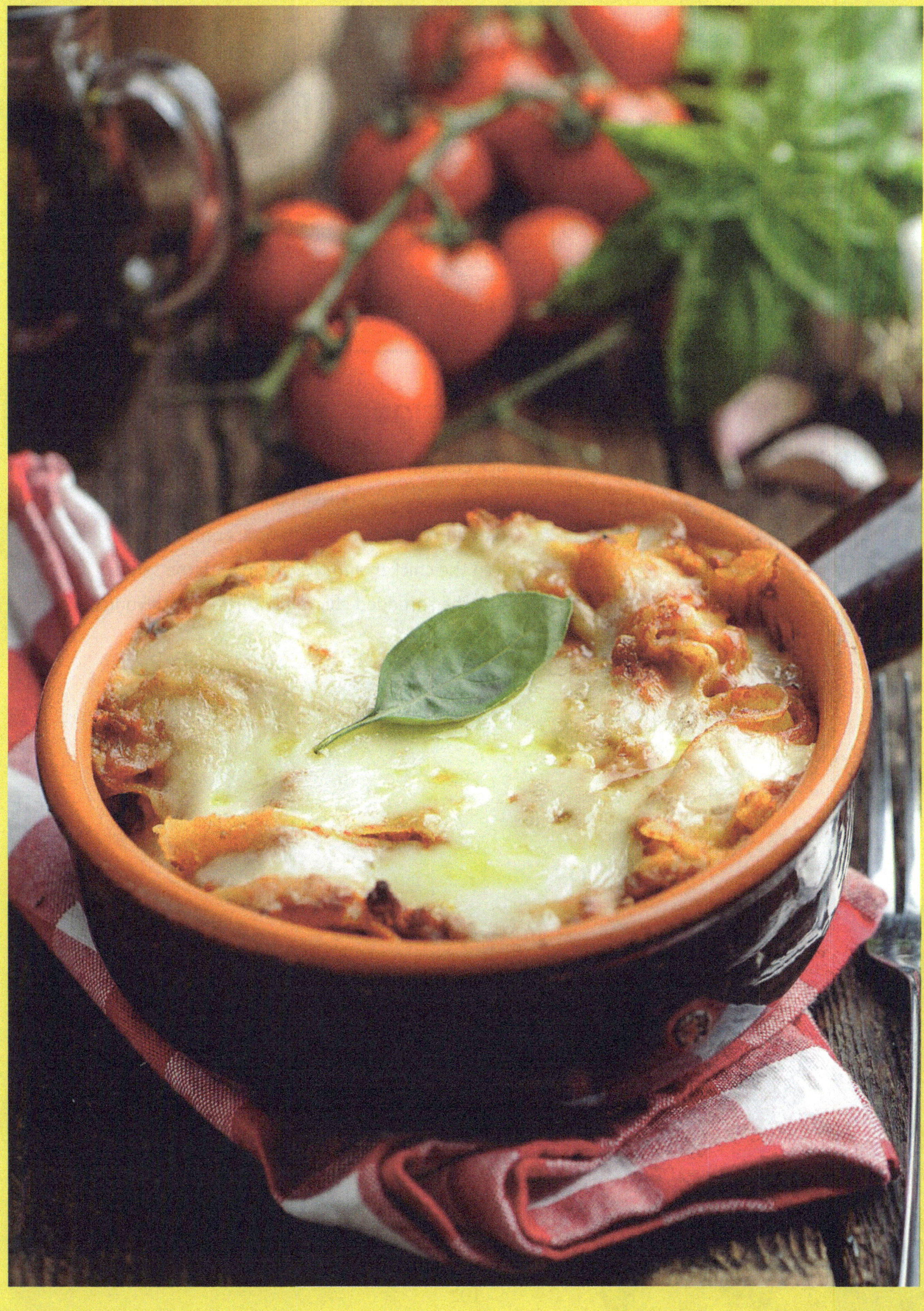

SLOW COOKER CHICKEN TACOS

Prep Time: 15 mins | **Cook Time:** 6 hours | **Serving:** 6

INGREDIENTS

- 2 lbs boneless, skinless chicken breasts
- 1 packet of taco seasoning
- 1 jar (16 oz) salsa
- Tortillas, for serving
- Toppings: shredded lettuce, diced tomatoes, shredded cheese, sour cream, avocado

INSTRUCTIONS

1. Place chicken breasts in the slow cooker. Sprinkle taco seasoning over the chicken and pour salsa on top.
2. Cover and cook on low for 6 hours until chicken is tender.
3. Shred the chicken and toss them with the sauce.
4. Serve the shredded chicken in tortillas with your choice of toppings.

Nutritional Values (per serving):

Calories: 220, Protein: 33g, Carbohydrate: 10g, Fat: 5g

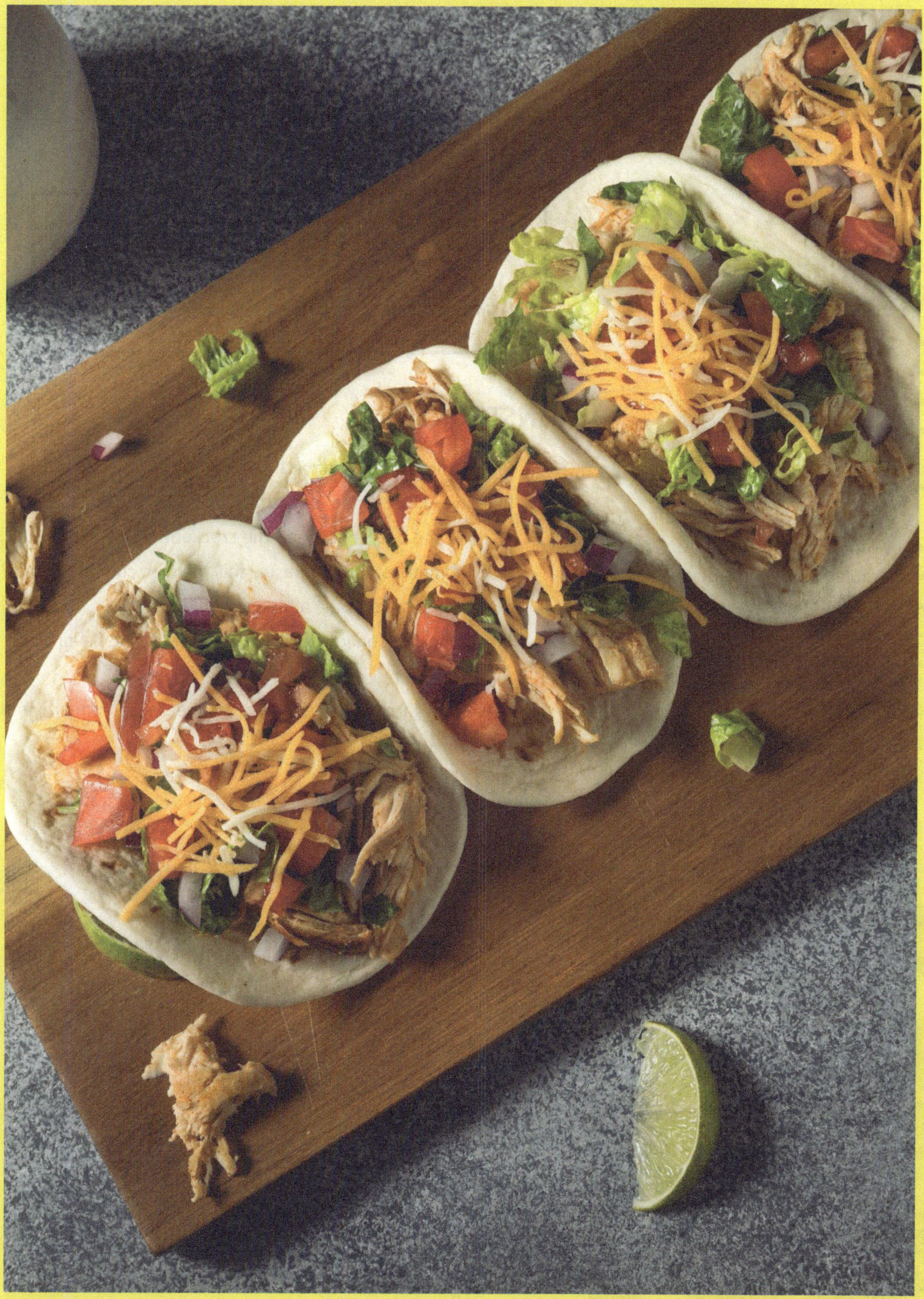

CROCKPOT BEEF CHILI

Prep Time: 20 mins   **Cook Time:** 8 hours   **Serving:** 8

INGREDIENTS

- 2 lbs ground beef
- 1 onion, chopped
- 2 cloves garlic, minced
- 2 cans (15 oz each weight) kidney beans, drained and rinsed
- 2 cans (14.5 oz each weight) of diced tomatoes, undrained
- 1 can (6 oz) tomato paste
- 2 tablespoons chili powder
- 1 teaspoon cumin
- 1 teaspoon salt
- 1/2 teaspoon black pepper

INSTRUCTIONS

1. Brown the ground beef with onion and garlic over medium heat in a skillet. Drain excess fat.
2. Transfer the beef mixture to the crockpot. Add kidney beans, diced tomatoes, tomato paste, chili powder, cumin, salt, and pepper. Stir to combine all the ingredients well.
3. Cover and cook on low for 8 hours, allowing the flavors to meld together.
4. Serve hot, garnished with shredded cheese, sour cream, and green onions.

Nutritional Values (per serving):

Calories: 400, Protein: 28g, Carbohydrate: 32g, Fat: 18g

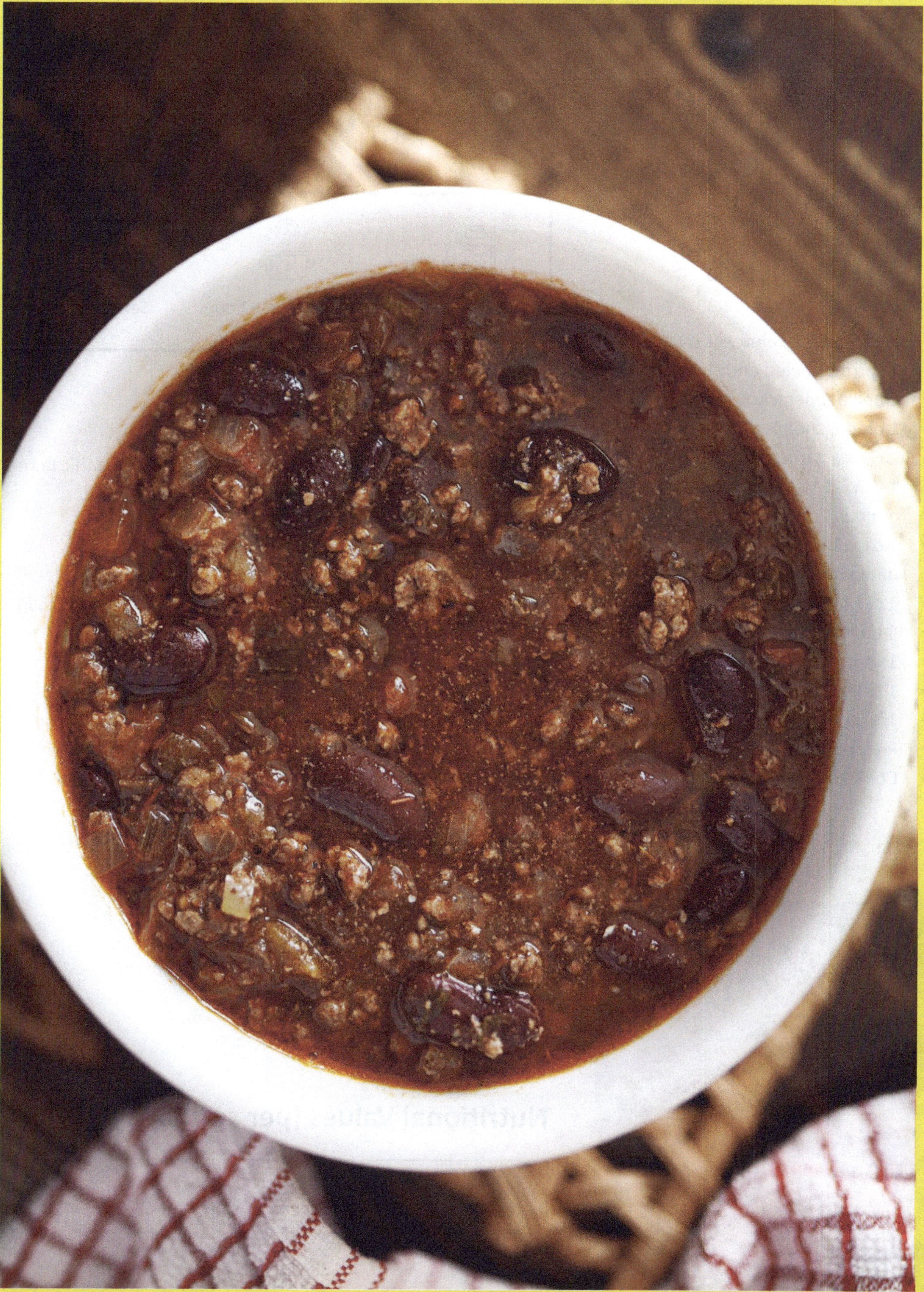

SLOW COOKER VEGETABLE CURRY

Prep Time: 20 mins   **Cook Time:** 6 hours   **Serving:** 6

INGREDIENTS

- 2 potatoes, peeled and diced
- 1 carrot, peeled and sliced
- 1 bell pepper, chopped
- 1 onion, chopped
- 2 cloves garlic, minced
- 1 can (15 oz weight) chickpeas, drained and rinsed
- 1 can (14.5 oz) diced tomatoes, undrained
- 1 can (13.5 oz) coconut milk
- 2 tablespoons curry powder
- 1 teaspoon ground ginger
- 1 teaspoon salt
- 1/2 teaspoon black pepper
- Fresh cilantro for garnish
- Cooked rice for serving

INSTRUCTIONS

1. Place potatoes, carrots, bell pepper, onion, and garlic in the slow cooker.
2. Add chickpeas and diced tomatoes with their juice.
3. Whisk together coconut milk, curry powder, ginger, salt, and pepper in a bowl. Drop this mixture over the vegetables in the slow cooker.
4. Stir to combine all the ingredients.
5. Cover and cook on low for 6 hours until vegetables are tender.
6. Serve the curry with cooked rice and fresh cilantro.

Nutritional Values (per serving):

Calories: 330, Protein: 9g, Carbohydrate: 44g, Fat: 14g

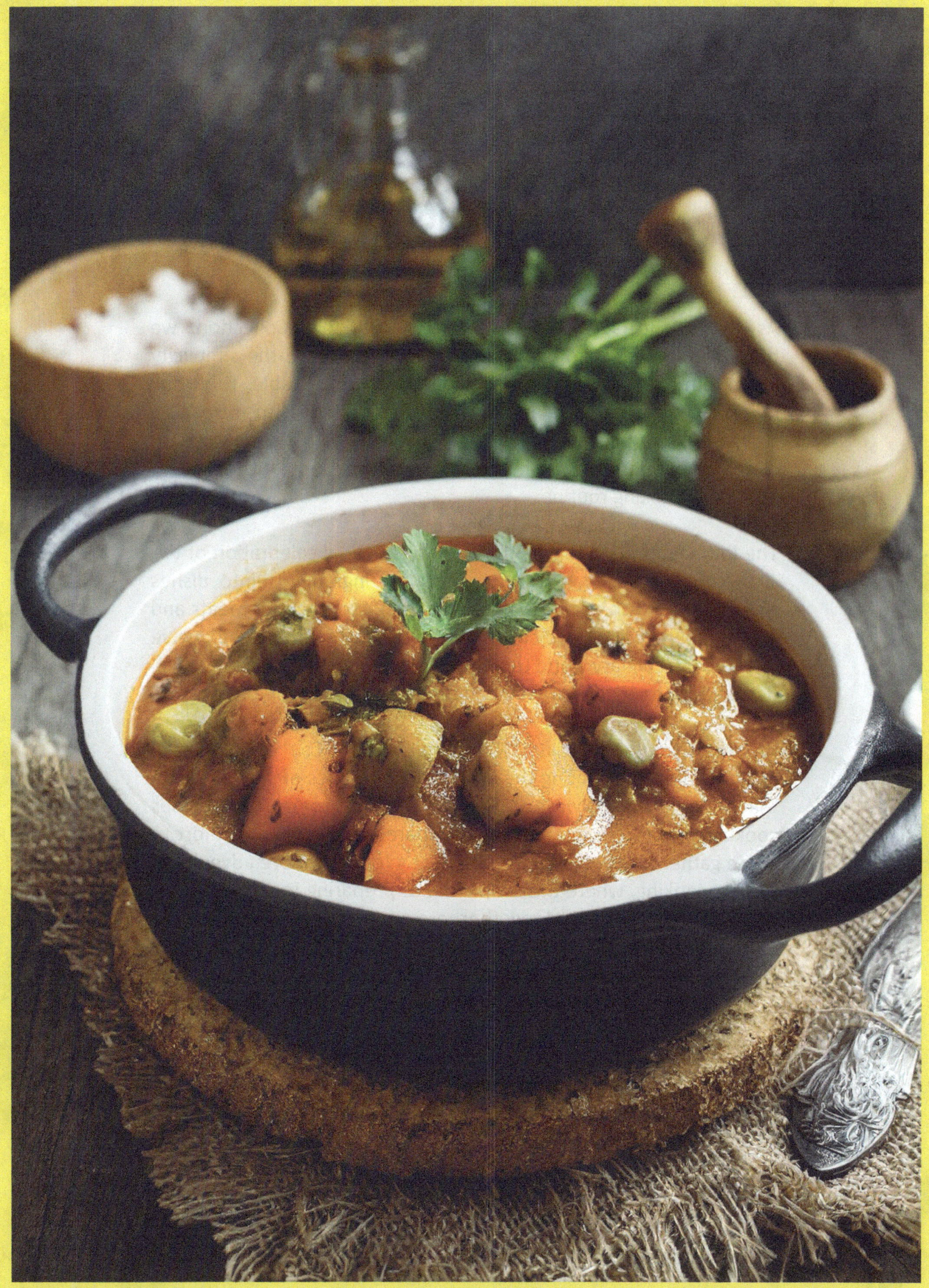

CONCLUSION

As we close the pages of "The Complete Slow Cooker Collection," we hope you feel inspired and empowered to embrace the simplicity and depth of flavor that slow cooking brings to the table. This book was crafted with a singular vision: to provide you with a treasure trove of savory, heartwarming meals that cater to a diverse range of tastes and preferences, all while ensuring ease and convenience in your daily cooking routine.

The journey through these 50 recipes has been a celebration of the slow cooker's ability to transform simple ingredients into dishes that resonate with comfort and satisfaction. From tender meats and robust stews to aromatic curries and hearty vegetarian fare, we've traveled the culinary world together, discovering the ease with which delicious, home-cooked meals can be a part of our everyday lives.

We thank you for choosing "The Complete Slow Cooker Collection" as your guide in exploring the limitless possibilities of slow cooking. May your kitchen always be filled with the aromas of delicious cooking, and may every meal you prepare bring joy and comfort to those gathered around your table. Here's to many more adventures in slow cooking, where the simple act of preparing food becomes a celebration of flavors and togetherness.

Thank you so much for reading this book and we hope you've enjoyed it, please consider some of the cookbooks in the following series

Book Series - Around the World in Tasty Ways:
https://geni.us/AroundTastyWaysSeries
Featuring cuisines from Spain, Italy, France, California, China and many more!

This collection of cookbooks brings the vibrant flavors of global cuisines right to your kitchen. From spicy Indian curries to savory Italian pastas, each book in this series explores a different corner of the world, offering authentic recipes and cultural insights. Whether you're craving the bold flavors of Paris or the delicate tastes of California, this collection has something for every palate. Join us on a journey of culinary discovery and explore the diverse and delicious cuisines of the world.

Book Series - Culinary Chronicles, Cooking with Passion:
https://geni.us/CulinaryChroniclesDL
Featuring Cuisines using Air Fryers, Grills, preparing appetizers, Dairy and Gluten free books too.
Introducing our diverse collection of cookbooks that revolutionize the way you approach meal preparation. Instead of focusing on specific countries, our collection delves into different styles of cooking and meal areas, ensuring a comprehensive exploration of culinary delights.

With our collection of cookbooks, you'll embark on a culinary adventure that transcends borders, bringing the world's flavors right to your kitchen. Whether you're entertaining guests or enjoying a cozy night in, these cookbooks are sure to inspire and delight.

View the full range of our publishing at our website
https://soreadytoread.com

For Cookbooks, Coloring, Technology and Self-development books or sport, there is something for everyone, of all ages, at **SoReadyToRead.com**

Sign up to our distribution list to be the first to discover new titles and promotions.

Made in the USA
Monee, IL
12 June 2024